DATE DUE

DEC 0 1 2008			
GAYLORD			PRINTED IN U.S.A.

MODERN WORLD
CULTURES

Africa South of the Sahara

◆

Australia and the Pacific

◆

East Asia

◆

Europe

◆

Latin America

◆

North Africa and the Middle East

◆

Northern America

◆

Russia and
the Former Soviet Republics

◆

South Asia

◆

Southeast Asia

◆

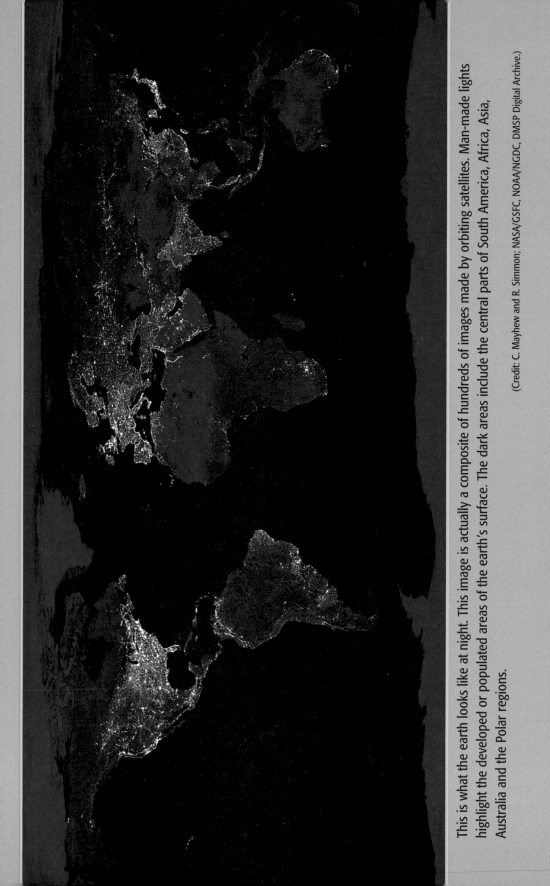

This is what the earth looks like at night. This image is actually a composite of hundreds of images made by orbiting satellites. Man-made lights highlight the developed or populated areas of the earth's surface. The dark areas include the central parts of South America, Africa, Asia, Australia and the Polar regions.

(Credit: C. Mayhew and R. Simmon; NASA/GSFC, NOAA/NGDC, DMSP Digital Archive.)

North Africa and the Middle East

Jeffrey A. Gritzner

University of Montana

and

Charles F. Gritzner

South Dakota State University

CHELSEA HOUSE
PUBLISHERS
An imprint of Infobase Publishing

#65820271   6/08

Cover: A man prays in front of a mosque in Iran.

North Africa and the Middle East

Copyright © 2006 by Infobase Publishing

Chelsea House
An imprint of Infobase Publishing
132 West 31st Street
New York NY 10001

Library of Congress Cataloging-in-Publication Data

Gritzner, Jeffrey A.
  North Africa and the Middle East / Jeffrey A. Gritzner, Charles F. Gritzner.
      p. cm. — (Modern world cultures)
  Includes bibliographical references and index.
  ISBN 0-7910-8145-1 (hardcover)
  1. Middle East—Juvenile literature. 2. Africa, North—Juvenile literature. I. Gritzner, Charles F.
II. Title. III. Series.
  DS44.G75 2006
  956—dc22   2006011649

Series and cover design by Takeshi Takahashi

Printed in the United States of America

Bang FOF 10 9 8 7 6 5 4 3 2 1

This book is printed on acid-free paper.

TABLE OF CONTENTS

Charles F. Gritzner

Geography is the key that unlocks the door to the world's wonders. There are, of course, many ways of viewing the world and its diverse physical and human features. In this series—modern world cultures—the emphasis is on people and their cultures. As you step through the geographic door into the 10 world cultures covered in this series, you will come to better know, understand, and appreciate the world's mosaic of peoples and how they live. You will see how different peoples adapt to, use, and change their natural environments. And you will be amazed at the vast differences in thinking, doing, and living practiced around the world. The modern world cultures series was developed in response to many requests from librarians and teachers throughout the United States and Canada.

As you begin your reading tour of the world's major cultures, it is important that you understand three terms that are used throughout the series: geography, culture, and region. These words and their meanings are often misunderstood. **Geography** is an age-old way of viewing the varied features of Earth's surface. In fact, it is the oldest of the existing sciences! People have always had a need to know about and understand their surroundings. In times past, a people's world was their immediate surroundings; today, our world is global in scope. Events occurring half a world away can and often do have an immediate impact on our lives. If we, either individually or as a nation of peoples, are to be successful in the global community, it is essential that we know and understand our neighbors, regardless of who they are or where they may live.

Geography and history are similar in many ways; both are methodologies—distinct ways of viewing things and events. Historians are concerned with time, or when events happened. Geographers, on the other hand, are concerned with space, or where things are located. In essence, geographers ask: "What is where, why there, and why care?" in regard to various physical and human features of Earth's surface.

Culture has many definitions. For this series and for most geographers and anthropologists, it refers to a people's way of life. This means the totality of everything we possess because we are human, such as our ideas, beliefs, and customs, including language, religious beliefs, and all knowledge. Tools and skills also are an important aspect of culture. Different cultures, after all, have different types of technology and levels of technological attainment that they can use in performing various tasks. Finally, culture includes social interactions—the ways different people interact with one another individually and as groups.

Finally, the idea of **region** is one geographers use to organize and analyze geographic information spatially. A region is an area that is set apart from others on the basis of one or more unifying elements. Language, religion, and major types of economic activity are traits that often are used by geographers to separate one region from another. Most geographers, for example, see a cultural division between Northern, or Anglo, America and Latin America. That "line" is usually drawn at the U.S.–Mexico boundary, although there is a broad area of transition and no actual cultural line exists.

The 10 cultural regions presented in this series have been selected on the basis of their individuality, or uniqueness. As you tour the world's culture realms, you will learn something of their natural environment, history, and way of living. You will also learn about their population and settlement, how they govern themselves, and how they make their living. Finally, you will take a peek into the future in the hope of identifying each region's challenges and prospects. Enjoy your trip!

Charles F. Gritzner
Department of Geography
South Dakota State University
May 2005

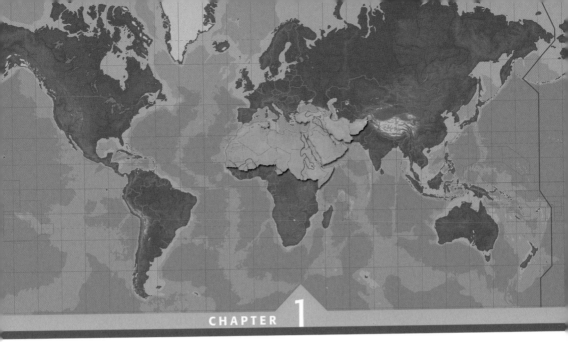

CHAPTER 1

A Diverse Environment

North Africa and the Middle East is a region of remarkable environmental diversity. It includes vast deserts, rugged mountains, windswept plateaus, bordering seas, and rivers that bring life to otherwise parched lands. The region's varied landscapes are matched by considerable contrasts in precipitation. Although most of the region receives less than 10 inches (250 millimeters) of precipitation annually, some areas of the Anatolian Peninsula receive more than 60 inches (1,500 millimeters). Despite the sparsely vegetated landscapes of much of North Africa and the Middle East, historical records document dramatic environmental change in recent centuries. At one time, many of the region's deserts, mountains, and plateaus were more heavily wooded and wildlife was more abundant. Today, however, some species, including the lion and tiger, have virtually disappeared from the region. Fortunately, several government-sponsored projects promote rehabilitation and species reintroduction.

North Africa and the Middle East is also a region of enormous historical importance. No region of the world has had a longer or more continuous history of human occupation, and none has contributed more to the modern world. Our earliest known human ancestor, *Sahelanthropus tchadensis*, roamed northern Africa some 7 million years ago. The region was among the first to witness the use of fire by humans. In addition, agriculture emerged on the floodplains of the Nile River about 18,500 years ago—with crops including lentils, chickpeas, wheat, barley, and dates. The region has long been recognized as a particularly important hearth of plant and animal domestication.

As a crossroads linking Asia, Africa, and Europe, North Africa and the Middle East is a region where ideas, materials, and technologies from distant lands were integrated into its cultures. This contributed to the emergence of remarkable ancient civilizations—Sumer and Akkad, Egypt, Canaan and Phoenicia, Babylonia, the Hittite Kingdom, Philistia, Assyria, Urartu (biblical Ararat), the kingdoms of the Hebrews and Aramaeans, and the Persian empires, to name only a few. Among their contributions to the modern world are urbanization, monotheistic religion, and several schools of philosophy. In addition, they contributed writing, mathematics, law, science, and important technological innovations, such as the wheel. The great Islamic caliphates and emirates of the Middle Ages were centers of art, science, and technology, at a time when Europe remained marginal to the civilized world. In the more recent past, as the Industrial Revolution transformed Europe, North Africa and the Middle East were held back by tradition. As a result, they gained neither the benefits nor the consequences of modernization. Today, more than two dozen countries are included within the borders of the region, with populations ranging from about 274,000 in Western Sahara to roughly 78,000,000 in Egypt.

Although every place on Earth's surface is unique, each shares characteristics with other places. Geographers refer to a grouping of similar places as a *region*. Today, North Africa and the Middle East would constitute a formal cultural region—an area in which the population shares cultural traits (practices), such as religion, language, or traditional livelihood systems. Islam, in its various forms, is the region's principal defining cultural trait. Arabic is the most widely spoken language, and it is the "official" language for roughly 276 million North Africans and Middle Easterners. Because much of North Africa and the Middle East is arid or semi-arid, pastoralism and irrigated agriculture are common rural economic activities. Urban centers are associated with transportation, trade, the manufacture of traditional goods, and various services. Cities and towns are typically centered around a large mosque (the Friday Mosque or *Masjid al-Jami*). Most also have associated schools, a public water supply, courts and administrative institutions, a citadel, and a commercial district—the vibrant and colorful *suq* (Arabic), *çarsi* (Turkish), or *bazaar* (Farsi). Beyond the central district are the residential "quarters"—closely knit, homogeneous communities where people live among others of the same ethnic group, religion, or village of origin.

The designation "North Africa and the Middle East" is admittedly cumbersome. Although North Africa is essentially that region of Africa between the Sahara Desert and Mediterranean coastal zone, the term *Middle East* has not enjoyed universal acceptance. Initially, the term referred to the lands of the Persian Gulf, an area positioned between the "Near East" and the "Far East" (from a West European perspective). Later, during World War II, the term was applied

Many cities and towns in North Africa and the Middle East are built around mosques, which serve as a place of public worship for Muslims. Pictured here is the Blue Mosque in Herat, Afghanistan, which is known for its beautiful cobalt blue and turquoise tile work.

to a British military province extending from Tripolitania (western Libya) to Iran. This province is still equated with the Middle East by many, but the cultural region discussed in this book is more extensive. It stretches from the Atlantic Ocean eastward, through the drylands of North Africa, and from the Anatolian and Arabian peninsulas eastward, through Iran—a distance of more than 4,000 miles (6,500 kilometers).

Despite the widely shared traits that define the region, North Africa and the Middle East possesses remarkable cultural diversity—indeed, the region has often been described as a cultural mosaic. Although Islam is the dominant religion, the majority Sunni sect shares the region with six major sects or offshoots of Shi'ism (the Imamis, Ismailis, Zaydis, Alawis, Druzes, and Ibadhis). Although there are many fewer Christians than Muslims in North Africa and the Middle East, surprisingly, there are a greater number of Christian sects. At least five have no outside affiliation. Five are affiliated with the Patriarchate of Constantinople. Six hold affiliation with the Roman Catholic Church, and there are numerous Protestant sects. The area is also home to several divisions of Judaism. Several other faiths, including Zoroastrianism and Bahaism, also emerged within the region.

Language is perhaps the most reliable indicator of culture, and the region has a rich diversity of tongues. Semitic (Arabic among others) and Hamitic (Afro-Asiatic family) languages are particularly widespread in North Africa, the Levant (eastern coastal region of the Mediterranean), and the borderlands of the Arabian Peninsula. Turkic (Altaic family) and various Indo-European languages are dominant in the northern and eastern areas of the region. In addition to Arabic, other widely spoken Semitic and Hamitic languages include Aramaic, Hebrew, Syriac, and Berber. The Turkic language also has many subtongues. Among the Indo-European languages are Farsi (Persian), Kurdish, Baluchi, Pashto, and Armenian (there are many others). Some Caucasic languages are also spoken in the region, as are less widely spoken languages such as Romany ("Gypsies") and Nubian. Obviously, as is suggested by the foregoing partial list of tongues, North Africa and the Middle East is a region of great linguistic diversity and complexity.

Throughout the region, many people still enjoy traditional livelihoods. Today, however, they are increasingly joined by competing and often conflicting trends in modernization and globalization. Development of the petroleum industry during the twentieth century has had a particularly great impact on traditional cultures. North Africa and the Middle East possesses more than 70 percent of the world's proven reserves of oil and correspondingly extensive reserves of natural gas. These reserves, however, are distributed unevenly within the region. Because of their dependency upon oil, industrialized countries that rely on petroleum have actively sought to gain access to the region's resources. In so doing, they have often influenced local governments, economies, educational systems, and cultural institutions. This has been particularly true of the industrialized countries of Europe and, since World War II, the United States. Hence, many in the region distrust Europeans and Americans. They reject Western models for development and actively engage in the restoration of traditional values and institutions. More and more, Islam serves as the organizational framework for the integration of social, economic, and political activity in North Africa and the Middle East.

Oil and natural gas are nonrenewable resources. Because demand is increasing at the same time that known reserves are being depleted, it is clear that petroleum-dependent economies cannot be sustained indefinitely. Hence, governments in North Africa and the Middle East are exploring alternative sources of energy and taking measures that would increase agricultural production. Like oil and natural gas, the water needed to support increased agricultural production is unevenly distributed. Because of the aridity (excessive dryness) that marks much of the region, the major rivers assume considerable importance. It is generally agreed that competition for the waters of the Nile, Jordan, Euphrates, Tigris, and other international rivers, as well as groundwater resources, might well serve as the basis for future disputes in the region.

Despite its fascinating landscapes, antiquities, diverse cultures, and perhaps because of its contested resources, North Africa and the Middle East is often associated with conflict. The region's problems include the Arab-Israeli conflict, Islamic fundamentalism, terrorism, and issues regarding the status of women. Creation of the Jewish state of Israel in 1948 produced cultural and political tensions that still plague the region. These tensions will continue until the pivotal issue of Palestine is satisfactorily resolved. Islamic fundamentalism increasingly opposes global popular culture and Western materialism. Much of the "terrorism" associated with the region essentially reflects growing resistance to Western intrusion into the region's social, economic, and political affairs. Women throughout much of the region may find greater security in tradition but fewer options for personal expression. Despite these issues and circumstances, North Africa and the Middle East is obviously much more than a region of strife and conflict. It is a region in which the past is prelude to the present. People "think historically" and attach great importance to the past. This trait contributes to the retention of culture, and the region remains a complex mix of languages, religions, livelihoods, and ethnic identities.

CHAPTER 2

The Natural Landscape

Nature dominates the landscape throughout much of North Africa and the Middle East. Because of its overwhelming importance, two chapters are devoted to the region's complex physical geography. This chapter focuses on landforms, soils, and water features; Chapter 3 is devoted to the weather and climate, natural vegetation, and animal life of the region.

LAND FEATURES

North Africa and the Middle East offers a great variety of landform features, surface characteristics, and human-use potentials. Plains and plateaus occupy much of the area, but mountain ranges tower over the landscape in some places. River valleys and their rich floodplains play

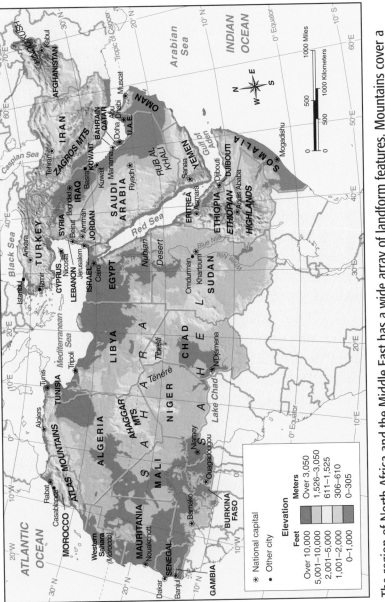

The region of North Africa and the Middle East has a wide array of landform features. Mountains cover a large portion of Afghanistan, Iran, and Turkey, while the vast Sahara Desert and Rub' al-Khali spread across North Africa and southern Saudi Arabia, respectively.

a prominent role in the region's settlement and economy, today as in the past.

Plains, Plateaus, and Desert Surfaces

Broad plains and plateaus are the region's dominant landform features. They cover much of North Africa, the Arabian and Anatolian peninsulas, and much of Iraq and Iran, and extend into southern Afghanistan. In areas where erosion has been particularly active, extensive hamadas (rock-strewn surfaces) are formed. Because water cannot penetrate through the basement rock formations, and sandstone is quite porous, many of the sandstone formations also serve as important aquifers that hold precious groundwater reserves. In contrast to the low-lying plains are the elevated plateaus of Anatolia and Iran.

Ergs (sand dunes, sand sheets, and undulating sand seas) are prominent features of the region's deserts. They are formed where sand and dust blown by the wind are deposited when the wind subsides. Among the most common types of dunes are tied dunes, which form in the lee (downwind side) of hills or other obstacles; parabolic blow-out dunes; crescent-shaped barchan and transverse dunes; longitudinal seifs; and the massive, complex forms associated with sand seas. Some dunes in the Sahara Desert attain heights of nearly 500 feet (150 meters); the mountainous sand ridges that dominate the ergs are said to reach 1,000 feet (305 meters) in height.

Rub' al-Khali (the Empty Quarter) in the southern interior of the Arabian Peninsula is the world's largest single concentration of dunes. An interesting phenomenon associated with desert dunes is their "singing," or booming. Such a serenade was recalled by R. A. Bagnold in his book *The Physics of Blown Sand and Desert Dunes*:

> On two occasions it happened on a still night, suddenly—a vibrant booming so loud that I had to shout to be heard by my companion. Soon other sources, set going by the

disturbance, joined their music to the first, with so close a note that a slow beat was clearly recognized. This weird chorus went on for more than five minutes continuously before silence returned and the ground ceased to tremble.

Various hypotheses have been advanced to explain the strange sounds, but the mystery remains unsolved. Although sand is most often associated with desert surfaces, its total area actually is relatively small, covering an estimated 10 to 15 percent of the region's surface.

More extensive than ergs are the regs or serirs (stony deserts) that occur in the region. Wind-scoured gravel often covers the surface. Mineralized solutions drawn to the surface by evaporation form a type of cement that binds the gravel into a hard, continuous sheet. These surfaces are referred to as "desert pavement." In addition, a dark coating of mineral compounds called "desert varnish" forms on the weathered rock surfaces. Although wind can shape desert landscapes, water, although relatively scarce, plays a much more important role in creating features of erosion and deposition. Other features of the region's deserts include basins that, after periods of precipitation, may hold temporary lakes.

Mountains

The plains and plateaus are bordered or intersected by mountain ranges. The most prominent ranges are ancient. They were formed by tectonic (mountain-building) forces millions of years ago resulting from the movement of tectonic plates. This movement is ongoing, and many of the mountains gradually increase in elevation.

In northwestern Africa, the Atlas Mountains extend from the Atlantic Ocean to northern Tunisia. They rise to an often snowcapped elevation of 13,665 feet (4,165 meters) at Jebel Toubkal in southwestern Morocco. Mountains also border the Red Sea, averaging 7,000 feet (2,135 meters) in the Hijaz range and reaching an elevation of 12,340 feet (3,760 meters) in Yemen. At the southeastern end of the Arabian Peninsula, Al Jabal al Akhdar (the Green Mountain) of Oman rises to 9,957 feet (3,035 meters) at Jabal ash Sham. The mountains bordering the Red Sea were created when tectonic forces separated the African and Arabian plates. When this occurred, a rift valley—a steep-sided trench between two parallel faults—was formed that today is occupied by the Red Sea. The rift system extends farther northward through the Gulf of Aqaba and Wadi al Arabah (a depression), to the Jordan River and Bekaa (al-Biqa') Valley. The Jordan River flows from Jabal ash Shaykh (Mount Hermon) southward, through the depression, into the Dead Sea, which, at 1,339 feet (408 meters) below sea level, is the lowest point on Earth's surface.

To the north and east of the mountains bordering the rift system are a number of major mountain ranges that radiate outward from the Armenian Knot in the rugged borderlands of Turkey, Iran, and the republics of the Caucasus region. The Taurus (7,000–9,000 feet; 2,135–2,745 meters) and Pontic (9,5000–13,000 feet; 1,524–3,962 meters) mountains extend westward through Turkey. The Elburz Mountains (12,000–15,000 feet; 3,660–4,575 meters) extend eastward through Iran, bordering the Caspian Sea. The Zagros Mountains (10,000–14,000 feet; 3000–4300 meters) extend southeastward through Iraq and Iran. Mount Ararat, which some believe to be the resting place of Noah's Ark, is the highest peak in the Armenian Knot, at 16,854 feet (5,137 meters).

In the Elburz Mountains of Iran, Mount Damavand towers to 18,612 feet (5,671 meters). Eastward from the Elburz is an almost continuous belt of mountains extending to the Pamir Knot—including the Kopeh Dagh, the Paropamisus Range, and the Hindu Kush. The Zard Kuh, in Iran, at 14,927 feet (4,548 meters), is the highest peak in the Zagros Mountains. Several mountain ranges, including the Makran and Sulaiman, extend eastward from the Zagros through

Baluchistan, then northward to the Pamir Knot. The mountains of the Pamir Knot are among the highest in the world. For example, Tirich Mir, located on the border of Afghanistan and northern Pakistan, rises to 25,239 feet (7,690 meters). The ranges extending eastward from the Elburz Mountains and the Zagros Mountains and their eastward extensions enclose three salt deserts: the Dasht-e Kavir and Dasht-e Lut in Iran, and Dasht-e Margo in Afghanistan.

Igneous (Volcanic) Activity

Volcanic mountains in this region were formed millions of years ago by forces set in motion by the movement of tectonic plates. The zones of structural weakness along these plate boundaries are also zones of igneous (volcanic) activity. These zones permit the upward movement of molten material (magma) from below Earth's surface. Of the various igneous processes, volcanoes are the most dramatic—often resulting in towering, snow-clad peaks. Mount Ararat and Mount Damavand, for example, are both volcanic peaks. Magma contains dissolved gases. If the gases are not vented into the atmosphere, violent volcanic eruptions can occur.

The most violent eruption in history occurred on the island of Thíra (present-day Santoríni) in the eastern Mediterranean Sea around 1500 B.C. The material spewed from the volcano was three or four times greater than that from Krakatoa in A.D. 1883, which itself exploded with the force of more than 10,000 Hiroshima-type atom bombs. Many believe that the eruption would have generated a *tsunami* with waves 330 feet (100 meters) high, and that the waves, along with the volcanic ash and poisonous gases released by the eruption, caused the collapse of the remarkable Minoan civilization on the island of Crete. Eighteenth-Dynasty Egyptian texts dating from around 1500 B.C. refer to a period of floods and darkness. Some scientists associate these events with the "days of darkness" of the Old Testament. Elsewhere, less dramatic fissure flows have given rise to plateaus and highlands in Yemen, Syria, and several other areas.

The Importance of Mountains in Arid Lands

As is true of mountains in the American West, the region's highlands are an important source of water. They are also areas of considerable biological diversity. For reasons explained in Chapter 3, mountains tend to be wetter and cooler than surrounding lowlands. Nearly all the rivers within North Africa and the Middle East begin in wetter highland regions and eventually flow across desert surfaces. Some rivers, such as the Nile, begin in mountains lying in more humid areas outside the region. Regardless of their origin, such streams play an extremely important role in the region's population, settlement, and economy. The greater moisture, temperature differences, and topographical diversity of mountain ranges result in many distinct ecological niches that provide nutrition and shelter for a variety of plants and animals. Hence, the biological diversity of mountainous areas is typically greater than that found on plains and plateaus.

Mountains also serve as areas of refuge for marginalized human populations. Because many groups that seek refuge in mountainous areas reside in relative isolation, they tend to retain their distinct languages, religions, and other aspects of culture. As a result, mountains of the region are both biologically and culturally diverse. The Druze and Kurds are among the many groups that have sought refuge in mountainous areas. Mountains also provide summer pasture for pastoral populations that practice transhumance, the moving of flocks to highland pastures in the spring of the year, then returning to the lowlands in the autumn. Historically, several North African and Middle Eastern mountains, such as Mount Ararat, have been of sacred importance to the societies of the region. The sacredness of mountains was also reflected in the construction of ziggurats (temple towers) as centers of worship

Throughout their culture's history, the Kurds have fought for their autonomy and because of this have often been subjugated and persecuted by other peoples. As a result, they often take refuge in mountainous regions, such as northern Iraq, where this family stands outside a refugee camp near Khalifan.

in Mesopotamian antiquity. More recently, the mountains of the region have acquired recreational importance, as trekking, skiing, and other alpine activities gain in popularity.

Earthquakes

Earthquakes occur frequently along the boundaries of tectonic plates in North Africa and the Middle East. Most are caused when a section of earth moves along a fault, which creates vibrations in the crust that travel as shock waves through the rock. When the waves reach the surface, they cause the earth to move in various ways—which is called seismic motion. Globally, it is estimated that more than 800,000 earthquakes are registered on seismographs annually. Most go unnoticed, but roughly 10 major earthquakes occur each year.

Many earthquakes occur in North Africa and the Middle East, and they often cause considerable loss of life. For example, the death toll of an earthquake that struck Aleppo (Halab), Syria, in 1138 was estimated at 230,000. Although death and destruction have been reduced somewhat by improvements in building construction, earthquakes remain a threat. About 43,200 individuals died in an earthquake that struck southeastern Iran in 2003, and more than twice that number perished in a 2005 earthquake that struck northern Pakistan and neighboring areas of Afghanistan and India. These tragedies were compounded by affecting thousands of others with serious injury, disease, and homelessness. It is obviously important that researchers develop dependable approaches for predicting earthquakes. Interestingly, earthquakes can sometimes be predicted by animal behavior. Many animals respond to the high-frequency sounds created by the moving rock by fleeing or otherwise acting abnormally.

MINERAL RESOURCES

North Africa and the Middle East is particularly well known for its considerable reserves of petroleum. Petroleum will be discussed elsewhere in the book, but other minerals are also of economic importance in the region. Four areas stand out as being of particular significance with regard to mineral resources: northwestern Africa, the Anatolian and Iranian plateaus, the ancient rocks that straddle the Red Sea, and the mountains of Oman.

Western Sahara, Morocco, and Algeria possess substantial deposits of iron ore, phosphate, and uranium. Anatolia and the plateau of Iran hold deposits of gold, silver, copper, chromite, zinc, iron ore, and bauxite, as well as coal and lignite. Lead and molybdenum are also found, together with a host of industrial minerals, such as boron, clays, pumice, and strontium. Egypt also possesses substantial deposits of coal and iron ore, and joins Algeria, Iran, and Turkey as a leading producer of pig iron and steel. Oman began developing its copper deposits in 1983 and ranks third in the region, after Iran and Turkey, in production.

Phosphate, used as an ingredient in chemical fertilizer, is an important mineral resource in North Africa and the Levant. Potash is also important, and both Israel and Jordan extract considerable quantities of the mineral from the Dead Sea. Salt is produced in almost every country of North Africa and the Middle East, but particularly large quantities are produced in Turkey, Iran, and Egypt. Deposits of precious and semiprecious stones, such as lapis lazuli and turquoise, are scattered throughout the region. The iron ore, coal and lignite, phosphate, gypsum, and pure limestone used in cement production are associated with sedimentary formations. Most metallic ores are associated with igneous intrusions in areas of intense tectonic activity.

Many of the region's minerals have been exploited for millennia. For example, iron ore was exploited by the Hittites of Anatolia prior to 1800 B.C. The gold deposits of western Turkey were historically associated with Croesus, the powerful king of Lydia, in the sixth century B.C. Cyprus was a principal source of copper in the ancient world. And the precious and semiprecious stones of the region have long been incorporated into the remarkable jewelry.

Soils

Soils are products of complex environmental interactions. Factors affecting soil development include parent material, climate, vegetation, microorganisms, landform relief, and time. In much of North Africa and the Middle East, aridity and heat play particularly important roles in soil formation. Aridity limits vegetation cover and soil organisms, thereby depriving soils of organic matter. High relief, such as rock outcrops and mountains, also affects soil development. Steep slopes require careful management in order to prevent severe erosion.

In many areas, particularly in southern Mesopotamia and the plateau of Iran, soil salinity (saltiness) is a serious problem.

Salinity also occurs in other areas in which crops are irrigated on poorly drained land or with water containing a high salt content. In some places, both drainage and water quality are issues. In the lowlands of Khuzestan, in Iran, for example, drainage is a serious problem, and the water of the Karun River contains high levels of salt during the dry season.

In most instances, the deserts of the region lack "true soils." Inadequate soil moisture prevents chemicals and other materials from leaching downward and creating the separate "horizons" by which soils are identified. In addition, with little organic matter, dryland soils are light in color. Soils suffering from salinization are similarly light in color. In the margins of the deserts, most soils have a high calcium content—in part because limestone is a widespread parent material in the region. These soils are often somewhat unproductive—particularly when caliche, a hard layer of calcium carbonate, is formed by solutions rising to the surface by capillary action when water evaporates. By and large, agriculture in arid lands is limited both by aridity and by the impact of aridity on soil development.

Nevertheless, the deltas and floodplains of the region's major rivers, as well as many other oases, contain highly productive soils. The fertile valley and delta region of the Nile has long been the world's largest and perhaps most productive oasis. There are also mature soils in many of the coastal plains and uplands of the northwestern and northern areas of the Middle East. These are areas in which precipitation typically exceeds 12 inches (300 millimeters). Particularly well-developed, productive soils are found in Asia Minor, western Iran, and the Fertile Crescent (the area composed of the Euphrates and Tigris rivers).

WATER FEATURES

Water resources of North Africa and the Middle East include a variety of seas and gulfs, rivers and streams, lakes, and groundwater. These bodies of water influence climate. They are also important economic assets: They produce fish and other aquatic resources, they are important shipping routes, and some lie over rich petroleum deposits.

Seas and Gulfs

The Red Sea and Gulf of Aden separate Africa from the Arabian Peninsula. They were created by seafloor spreading. Tectonically, the Red Sea is a northward extension of Africa's Great Rift Valley and reaches depths of 6,500 feet (2,000 meters) in its main trough. Because the rift is a zone of structural weakness, magma is able to flow upward into the floor of the sea, heating the seawater. This has resulted in the formation of hot brines and the development of sludge containing high concentrations of zinc, copper, silver, gold, and other metals. Sudan and Saudi Arabia have formed the Red Sea Commission, a body that will determine how best to share this potentially important resource.

The Persian Gulf lies in a tectonically downfolded basin and is relatively shallow. It reaches depths of more than 330 feet (100 meters) near the Strait of Hormuz, but its average depth is only 115 feet (35 meters). Because the waters of the gulf are shallow and subject to considerable evaporation, they are warm and highly saline. In some areas of the gulf, the salinity is as high as 7 percent, or twice the average for seawater worldwide. At one time, the Persian Gulf was the world's most important source of pearls; it is now a major source of petroleum.

The Mediterranean Sea is partially a remnant of the ancient Tethys Sea and was created in part by a collapsed structure along the zone in which the African and Eurasian plates are colliding. Its greatest depth, 15,072 feet (4,594 meters), is near Crete. The sea has long served as an important fishery and a marine highway linking North Africa, Asia, and Europe.

The Black Sea (the Euxine Sea of antiquity) reaches depths of more than 7,000 feet (2,135 meters) along its southern margin. Because rivers and streams, including major rivers such as the Dnieper, flow into it, the sea is only moderately brackish. Recent discoveries indicate that the Black Sea basin was a major center of agricultural activity in antiquity. However, some 7,500 years ago, when the continental glaciers of the ice age melted and sea levels rose, water again flooded the basin, and agricultural production was greatly affected.

Rivers

Although many of the watercourses in North Africa and the Middle East originate in nearby highlands, some of the most important rivers are exotic—streams that flow throughout the year from a wetter distant location. The branches of the Nile River, for example, rise in the distant mountains and plateaus of East Africa, join in Sudan, and then flow northward through the drylands of North Africa to the Mediterranean Sea. With a length of 4,240 miles (6,825 kilometers), the Nile is the world's longest river. The region's other major river system is the Tigris-Euphrates. The Tigris and Euphrates rivers rise in the Anatolian highlands and Zagros Mountains. The principal branches of the system join in southern Iraq and flow into the Persian Gulf through the Shatt al-Arab. The Tigris is some 1,150 miles (1,850 kilometers) in length; the Euphrates is roughly 1,700 miles (2,700 kilometers) long. Although the Euphrates is longer, the Tigris carries 25 percent more water.

The Nile Valley and Mesopotamia (as well as the Indus Valley, in South Asia's arid Pakistan) were major hearths of ancient civilization—the so-called hydraulic civilizations. These civilizations shared a dependency on irrigated agriculture. Many of these systems were highly productive. It is widely believed that an agricultural surplus freed some farmers to become specialists in other activities, and that the increased social complexity led to the rise of these ancient civilizations.

Many smaller rivers are of considerable local importance as sources of domestic water, irrigation, and hydroelectric power. Several flow from the Atlas Mountains of North Africa, the highlands of Anatolia, and western Iran. Three rivers in the Levant have significance far beyond their size: The Jordan River has headwaters draining southeastern Lebanon, southwestern Syria, and northern Israel. Its principal tributary, the Yarmuk, enters the Jordan just south of the Sea of Galilee. Waters of the Jordan are declining in quantity and deteriorating in quality, and this issue is hotly contested by the countries of the Jordan basin (particularly water-starved Israel and Jordan). Many streams are wadis, intermittent water courses that flow only briefly after periods of rain, or seasonally. Several large wadis flow from the Atlas Mountains and coastal highlands of North Africa and from the mountains and plateaus of Middle Eastern drylands. Some are remnants of drainage systems formed during more humid periods of the past. Others were formed by the sudden discharge of historically documented storms—such as the flood that destroyed Tamanrasset in the central Saharan Ahaggar Mountains in 1922.

Lakes

With the exception of the Caspian Sea, there are relatively few natural freshwater lakes of any size or significance in North Africa and the Middle East. Among the most prominent lakes of the region are the Sea of Galilee and the Dead Sea. The Sea of Galilee's surface covers only 64 square miles (165 square kilometers). It has a maximum depth of 138 feet (42 meters), and its surface is some 710 feet (214 meters) below mean sea level. The sea has both religious and historical significance, as well as contemporary economic and political importance. Christians attach particular importance to the Sea of Galilee because of its association with the teachings of Jesus Christ. It now serves as the control basin for Israel's national water system.

The Jordan River flows into the Dead Sea, which is located farther to the south. It has a maximum depth of 1,300 feet (400 meters). At more than 1,339 feet (408 meters) below sea level, the surface of the Dead Sea is the lowest body of water on Earth. Like other lakes with no outlets, the Dead Sea has become increasingly saline, because of evaporation from its

The Dead Sea, which lies between Jordan and Israel, is a saltwater lake located at the lowest point on Earth (1,339 feet, or 408 meters, below sea level). Due to its warm water and salinity—more than eight times that of the ocean—the lake is a popular tourist destination, where bathers can comfortably float on the surface.

surface. Additional salt is added by saline springs that contribute to its water volume.

Many lakes, such as those of Mesopotamia, are shallow and little more than marshes. More significant are the larger saltwater lakes that occupy broad basins on the Anatolian plateau and in northwestern Iran. The largest are Lake Van and Lake Urmia, both of which were of great importance to various ancient kingdoms in the region. Lake Van reaches a depth of 82 feet (25 meters) and covers 1,434 square miles (3,714 square kilometers). Lake Urmia is only 60 feet deep (18 meters), with a maximum surface of 2,317 square miles (6,000 square kilometers). The lake is very salty. Additional salt lakes, such as Daryacheh-ye Namak, are found on the plateau of Iran, and Daryacheh-ye Sistan on the Iran-Afghanistan frontier is another lake of regional importance.

As noted earlier, the Caspian Sea is actually a large lake. It has no outlet, and its surface is roughly 92 feet (28 meters) below sea level. It reaches depths of 3,363 feet (1,025 meters) in the southwestern part of its basin and, like the Black Sea, is fed by large rivers from the north. It is only moderately brackish. The Caspian Sea is well known as a source of Iranian and Russian caviar—the valuable pickled roe (eggs) of the sturgeon. It is also well known as a source of petroleum. Commercial exploitation of petroleum in the Caspian basin began in the 1870s, and the basin remains economically and strategically important. With the collapse of the Soviet Union in 1991, the basin's petroleum has been contested by Iran, Azerbaijan, Russia, Kazakhstan, and Turkmenistan. This competition has become an important component of American and European strategies to assure access to this vital resource. Pollution from agricultural activity and the exploitation of petroleum is threatening the aquatic resources of the Caspian, and widespread poaching further endangers the valuable sturgeon.

Groundwater

Groundwater also serves the needs of North African and Middle Eastern populations. The water is found in two major types of aquifers (deposits). Shallow surface aquifers are found along river valleys and beneath plains and alluvial fans. They are typically unconfined, small, and have water tables (upper level of the aquifer) that respond rapidly to local precipitation. The second type is deep, extensive, and generally composed of sandstone and limestone. Many of these aquifers contain water accumulated during more humid periods in the distant past. Aquifers are sources of water for wells and for the remarkable subterranean aqueducts (*qanats, karez, foggaras*) that have provided water for North African and Middle Eastern communities for thousands of years.

As indicated earlier, a reliable source of water is essential to human survival. Dependable water sources have therefore played important roles in the region's settlement and economic activity. In the past, water typically supported domestic and agricultural needs at the local level. With population increase, particularly the rapid growth of cities, local water resources are often unable to satisfy the growing demand. As a result, there are an increasing number of large-scale water-supply projects, such as Turkey's Southeast Anatolia Project (better known as GAP, based on its Turkish name, Güneydo u Anadolu Projesi) on the Tigris and Euphrates rivers. The project includes 22 large dams constructed to provide water for irrigated agriculture and electricity to satisfy the country's growing demand for energy. The project is designed to irrigate 4.2 million acres (1.7 million hectares) and generate 27 billion kilowatt hours of electricity annually—roughly 25 percent of Turkey's energy needs.

Wells and subterranean aqueducts have long supported the activities of oasis populations and others without ready access to surface water. In recent years, however, groundwater has also been exploited for some large regional projects as well. For example, Libya's $25-billion (in U.S. dollars) Great Man-Made River Project draws water from ancient aquifers beneath the Sahara Desert. Unfortunately, in the drylands of North Africa and the Middle East, groundwater use often exceeds the rate of recharge. The Great Man-Made River Project draws on both "fossil water" and groundwater that slowly seeps northward from the Lake Chad basin. Few projects of this kind have been sustainable. The region's drylands are littered with dry wells and decaying aqueducts. Some oases are no longer able to support significant populations. Widespread use of high-volume mechanized pumps has aggravated the problem.

Unfortunately, almost all large-scale projects in the region have met with mixed results. The fifth-century-B.C. Hippocratic essay, "On Airs, Waters, and Places," discussed relationships between water quality and human well-being. Unfortunately, in the modern world, more attention is paid to the quantity of water, rather than to its quality. Several projects have increased the incidence of diseases such as schistosomiasis (a parasitic disease). Many also have caused salinization or other problems resulting in a loss of agricultural productivity. Agricultural chemicals, water-temperature change, and other factors have affected fisheries and related aquatic resources.

As the demand for water grows, the waters of international rivers are increasingly contested by the countries through which they flow. For example, Turkey's GAP reduces the downstream water in the Tigris and Euphrates rivers available for irrigation and energy production in Syria and Iraq. Egypt's needs are threatened by planned projects in the upper-basin states of the Nile River. The diminishing waters of the Jordan River basin are contested among Israel, Jordan, and the Palestinians, as well as Syria and Lebanon. It is believed by many that future competition for increasingly scarce water resources will result in armed conflict, much as competition for petroleum does today.

CHAPTER 3

Climate and Ecosystems

Weather (day-to-day conditions of the atmosphere) and climate (long-term average weather) are the most important environmental elements of North Africa and the Middle East. Wind and moving water erode and redeposit earth materials, forming unique landscapes. Soils are influenced by conditions of temperature and precipitation. Streams and lakes depend on moisture, as do plants and animals. People, of course, are also highly dependent on moisture.

Technically, an ecosystem includes all elements of the natural environment that in various ways interact with one another. In this chapter, consideration will be given only to weather and climate and the region's plant and animal life.

WEATHER AND CLIMATE

Weather and climate have a considerable impact on people and their activities. They influence where people live, their dwellings, and the clothes they wear. Temperature and moisture also establish practical limits to outdoor labor, the crops that can be grown, and many other aspects of life.

The latitudinal location of a place determines the angle at which the sun's rays strike Earth's surface, thus determining the amount of solar radiation received. Further, as the vertical rays of the sun shift with the seasons, belts of atmospheric pressure and winds change accordingly. The arid southern zone of the region (which is south of the 35th parallel) lies under a subtropical high-pressure belt during much of the year. Air in the belt heats and dries as it descends. Once the descending air reaches Earth's surface, it flows northward and southward. The northward flow joins the belt of the prevailing westerly winds. The southward flow veers counterclockwise to become the northeast trade winds. The dry high pressure produces a desert belt extending from the Atlantic Ocean eastward through the Sahara to the deserts of Arabia, Iran, Afghanistan, and on into Pakistan and western India.

The more humid areas north of the 35th parallel, extending from the Aegean and Mediterranean seas to northern Iran, are chiefly a transitional zone between pressure belts. They experience a Mediterranean climate similar to that of Southern California. Here, summers tend to be warm and dry and winters cool and relatively moist. The summers are dry because the high-pressure system that contributes to desert conditions farther south expands to cover the region of Mediterranean climate. During the winter, the same zone lies under a belt of stormy prevailing westerly winds and atmospheric depressions that migrate southward. Hence, latitude and the changing position of belts of atmospheric pressure strongly influence the Mediterranean climate.

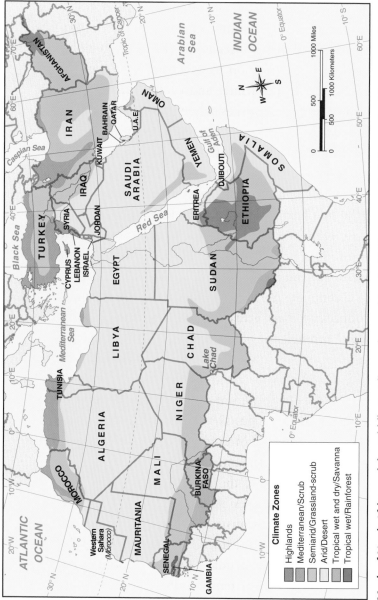

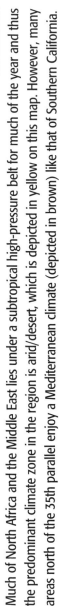

Much of North Africa and the Middle East lies under a subtropical high-pressure belt for much of the year and thus the predominant climate zone in the region is arid/desert, which is depicted in yellow on this map. However, many areas north of the 35th parallel enjoy a Mediterranean climate (depicted in brown) like that of Southern California.

Relationships between land and water also influence climate. Large bodies of water, such as the Mediterranean Sea, are major sources of moisture. When located on the windward side (the side facing the wind) of a landmass, they increase the potential for precipitation and humidity. Such bodies of water also moderate air temperature. Because of the relative stability of water temperatures in relation to those on land, warming onshore winds occur in the winter and cooling winds occur during the summer. This moderates temperatures in the coastal zones throughout the region.

Topography also influences weather and climate. Temperatures decrease with increased elevation; therefore, mountainous areas and plateaus experience cooler conditions than do the surrounding plains. Mountain ranges also intercept moisture-laden winds, resulting in precipitation on their windward side.

Latitude, pressure systems, land-water relationships, and landforms combine to produce weather conditions such as temperature, winds, and precipitation. This, in turn, produces climates specific to certain areas: deserts, steppes, and more humid temperate zones.

Temperature

Throughout North Africa and the Middle East, summer temperatures are relatively high. The highest mean daily temperatures during this period, in excess of 86°F (30°C), occur in the southern deserts. Daytime temperatures are often extremely high. For example, the highest temperature ever recorded, 136°F (58°C), was at Al 'Aziziyah, Libya, on September 13, 1922. Fortunately, the diurnal (daily) temperature range is also considerable. Because the heat accumulated during the day is radiated back into the cloudless sky and dry air during the night, predawn minimum temperatures are often quite low. The diurnal temperature range (range between highs and lows) for many interior cities in the region is about 35 to 40°F (20–22°C). For example, in Damascus, Syria, a typical July daytime high might be 100°F (38°C), accompanied by a nighttime low of 64°F (18°C). In coastal regions, diurnal temperature ranges tend to be smaller than in the interior.

Although summer temperatures are generally high throughout North Africa and the Middle East, there are greater contrasts within the region during the winter. January temperatures in the region's northern zone can be severe—particularly in the high plateaus and mountains. For example, the average January maximum temperature at Erzurum in eastern Anatolia (Turkey) is 22°F (−5.5°C); the average minimum is 8°F (−13°C). In the region's southern zone, average temperatures are well above freezing. The average January maximum daily temperature in Riyadh, Saudi Arabia, for example, is 70°F (21°C); the average minimum is 46°F (8°C).

Wind

During the summer months, a relatively simple pattern of low pressure exists, and winds are gentle. Nevertheless, quite persistent winds can develop in some areas, blowing toward the center of low-pressure cells. In the Tigris-Euphrates lowlands, such a wind, known as the *shamal*, is a dry north or northwesterly wind that blows throughout much of the summer. A similar, but more forceful wind, the *bad-e sad-o-bist* (120-day wind), affects much of southeastern Iran. Along the Mediterranean coast, land-sea breezes are well developed during the summer. During the day, air pressure over the sea is greater than that over land, resulting in onshore winds and cooler, more humid conditions in coastal areas. Because the land cools more rapidly than the sea at night, the pressure relationships are reversed. Air pressure is higher over the land and lower over the warmer water, and offshore winds occur.

It is more difficult to speak of average conditions during the winter. The region is crossed by a succession of high- and low-pressure systems that develop over Anatolia and the plateau of Iran as a result of very cold winter temperatures. The steep pressure gradients (differences in pressure between high- and low-pressure systems) produce the various local winds for which the region is so well known. For example, hot, dry winds with differing local names (*khamsin* in Egypt, *jibli* in Libya, *shlur shluq* in Syria and Lebanon, *sharqi* in Iraq, and *simoon*—the "poisonous" winds of Iran) occur when tropical continental air from over North Africa and Arabia is drawn into the region by traveling cyclones—small tropical low-pressure systems. These winds are strong, and often give rise to severe dust or sand storms. In the fifth century B.C., Greek historian Herodotus recorded the fate of a Persian army that set out from Egypt against a rising south wind to subdue Siwa Oasis. The Persians lost their way and were never heard from again. In some cultures, the winds are believed to affect one's behavior, so people are not held accountable for errors of judgment if the wind is howling!

The winds of North Africa and the Middle East have an important impact on the region. They are responsible for the shifting sands and for respiratory complaints, and are a significant agent of erosion. For millennia, they also influenced patterns of commerce—seasonally changing winds affected both the caravan trade and navigation under sail. For example, in Egypt, steady northeasterly trade winds permit *faluqas* (Nile River boats) to sail upstream against the current. They then furl their sails and drift downstream on the return trip. In the Red Sea, the seasonal northeasterly trade winds prevented sailing craft from traveling northward beyond Ras Banas, Egypt, near the Tropic of Cancer. Trade was then carried over land to the Nile and, again, the currents of the river offset the contrary winds, as the trade goods traveled northward.

Farther to the east, strong summertime southwesterly monsoon winds draw water away from the southern shore of the Arabian Peninsula, causing an upwelling of cool water and improved conditions for fishing. Seasonal winds also influence agricultural activity, military planning—including planning for the recent conflicts in the Persian Gulf region—and architectural design. In southern Iran and the gulf coasts, for example, a feature of many of the older houses is the *badgir*, the so-called Persian wind tower that directs air downward into the rooms below.

Precipitation

Aridity is the dominant natural feature of North Africa and the Middle East. Of all the countries in the region, only two, Turkey and Lebanon, possess no areas of extreme aridity—areas in which precipitation is below 8 inches (200 millimeters) during the year. In the extensive southern deserts of the region, precipitation averages less than four inches (100 millimeters) annually. Within the region, contrasts are considerable. For example, Dakhla, in the Libyan Desert, averages only a trace of precipitation, whereas Rize, on the Turkish Black Sea coast, has received as much as 158 inches (4,045 millimeters) in a single year. In southern Arabia, humid monsoon air gives rise to the summer maximum of rainfall in Yemen and Zufar, in southern Oman.

It is said that water is life. Hence, patterns of precipitation are of critical importance. They strongly influence the nature of environmental and rural livelihood systems. Rain-fed agriculture can be practiced in areas of dependable precipitation, such as much of Anatolia and the Caspian lowlands, and in the mountains of the region. Most agriculture, however, depends on irrigation systems fed by the diversion of watercourses flowing from areas of higher precipitation or by groundwater. In those areas most hostile to cultivation, pastoralism (raising livestock) becomes a prominent economic activity. The forms of livestock included in pastoral systems also reflect the availability of water. For example, when it is hot, cattle require considerable water—as their internal temperature is regulated by water passing through their bodies. They are poorly adapted to desert environments. Camels, on the other hand, retain water when stressed by heat and can live in areas with little available water. Goats, sheep, and donkeys are also relatively well adapted to the drylands of the region.

Thanks largely to their ability to survive without food and water for extended periods of time, camels are used throughout much of North Africa and the Middle East not only to transport goods but also to provide milk, meat, and wool. Pictured here is a Jordanian shepherd preparing to sell one of his camels at a livestock market near Amman.

In most of North Africa and the Middle East, potential evapotranspiration (loss of moisture by evaporation from the land and transpiration from vegetation) exceeds the amount of water received through precipitation. Nevertheless, almost all areas, except the most severely arid, have periods of water surplus and water deficit.

PLANT AND ANIMAL LIFE

Vegetation of North Africa and the Middle East roughly mirrors the region's dominant climatic zones. Dryland vegetation is noteworthy for its many interesting adaptations to unreliable precipitation. These are seen in root structure, such as deep tap roots and shallow roots that spread widely from the plant; in a broad range of physiological adaptations, such as small leaves; in location, to maximize moisture availability and minimize water loss through transpiration; and in reproductive strategies, including seed viability that can last for centuries. Many of the nonwoody seed-bearing plants mature rapidly. Some germinate within 3 days of adequate rainfall and sow their seeds within 10 or 15 days of germination.

Desert tree and shrub species include the umbrella-shaped thorn acacia and camelthorn, date palms, and jujube. Salt-tolerant species (halophytes), such as tamarisk, are found in coastal areas and in the salt deserts. Several grasses and herbs also are found within the region. These play a very important role in regional economies, because they form important seasonal pastures. Also of interest and local importance are edible fungi, such as desert truffles.

During the ice age, much of the region received far more moisture than it does today and supported plant life common today in more humid areas. Sheltered in some mountain areas are occasional "island" stands of relict vegetation—species that are long gone from the surrounding desert landscapes. These exotic plants serve as reminders of the desert's complex vegetation history. They also provide valuable clues to the much greater ecological diversity of the recent past when conditions were much wetter. Prominent among the relict species of the desert highlands are varieties of olive and cypress.

Desert animals also possess various means of conserving moisture. For example, insects obtain liquids by feeding either on vegetation or on other insects. Some have watertight outer coverings that prevent water loss. Many birds, reptiles, and small mammals, such as the fennec fox, obtain their food and liquid by consuming insects. Particularly interesting is the survival mechanism of the desert snail. In the absence of water, desert snails become dormant and often remain inactive for several years before being revived by rainfall. They also serve as important sources of food for birds and animals, their shells providing dietary calcium. Many large mammals, such as gazelles, take advantage of available shade and possess physiological mechanisms that permit them to retain body liquid when stressed. Some desert animals, such as the addax, rarely need to drink at all. (Humans also avoid the heat of the day; they have developed loose clothing, tents, and thick-walled houses that permit them to live in the deserts of the region.)

As is true of the relict flora (vegetation), the relict fauna (animals) of the region's drylands underscores the dramatic changes that have taken place. Tropical catfish and other species can still be found in the waters of isolated oases. The cobras of the northern Sahara are similarly of tropical origin. Pygmy crocodiles were found in scattered pools as recently as the 1980s in Mauritania. They may still exist in the remote pools of the Tibesti Mountains of Chad. These, of course, are artifacts of an earlier age. More subtle has been the progressive loss of well-adapted, more mobile species to hunting and habitat destruction. Although the North African elephant became extinct during the Roman period, lions, ostrich, and a broad range of other species were still established in the northern margins of the Sahara as late as 1830. The last of the northern addax (a large antelope), a herd of 20 animals, was destroyed by a hunting party in the early 1920s. Among the species still found in the drylands are gerbils, hares, hedgehogs, weasels, and mongooses. There are also Barbary sheep, gazelles, and wild donkeys. Monkeys and baboons can be found in some wooded areas. Predators include hyenas, jackals, foxes, and wildcats. The many domesticated animals of North Africa and the Middle East include goats, sheep, camels, cattle, horses, and donkeys.

The desert is home to many varieties of insects. Flies and mosquitoes are commonplace and a nuisance almost everywhere. There are bees, dragonflies, butterflies, and locusts; ants and termites are omnipresent pests in many locations. Then there are the much less welcome insects and arachnids—ticks, lice, scorpions, and centipedes, and, of course, many spiders and beetles.

Bird life, including both resident and migratory populations, is abundant and includes more than 500 species. The coastal zones and interior waterways attract many species of water and shore birds. There are also vultures, falcons, bustards; sandgrouses, pigeons, and doves; owls; larks, swallows, and wagtails; ravens; and nightingales, warblers, and sparrows. Frogs and toads are associated with the lakes and pools of the deserts. Lizards, horned vipers, and other reptilian species are found among the rocks and dunes. Catfish, chromy, and other fish are found in the lakes and pools, and brine shrimp and other crustaceans are important links in the short food chains of the deserts. The surrounding seas of North Africa and the Middle East are rich in sardines, tuna, and other species— particularly in the cool waters in areas of upwelling.

Vegetation of the cooler semidesert region includes grasses and robust plants. Wildlife includes hedgehogs, hares, and gophers, as well as wolves, jackals, and hyenas. The bird life is similar to that of the warmer drylands. The short-grass steppes include some broadleaf trees found along watercourses, and animal species, including gazelles, wild pigs, jackals, and hyenas. Coursers, plovers, and flamingos are among the birds of the steppes. The vegetation of the semidesert includes short grasses and woody perennials, such as tamarisk. The wildlife is similar to that in the short-grass steppes but, in the eastern margins of the region, also includes elements of the Indian fauna, such as the leopard, cheetah, and macaque (short-tailed monkey).

As one might expect, mountainous areas of the region contain a diversity of ecological conditions and a corresponding diversity of wildlife. Among the large cats of the mountains are various types of leopards, jungle cats, caracal, and lynx. Other carnivores include the wolf, jackal, fox, hyena, mongoose, polecat, ferret, weasel, otter, badger, and brown bear. Among the herbivores are gazelle, ibex, several types of wild sheep, red deer, and wild pig. The rhesus monkey is found in Afghanistan. Other animals include several species of hedgehogs, shrews, hares, pikas, squirrels, gophers and groundhogs, porcupines, rats and mice, jerboas, gerbils, and voles. There are also several species of bats.

The region is home to many bird species, including some 80 types of wild pigeons and doves. A large number of waterfowl arrive during the course of their spring and autumn migrations. These include several species of ducks, geese, pelicans, and swans. There are also shore birds, such as snipes, plovers, herons, storks, and cranes. The bird life of the mountains and plateaus is diverse, and several species are hunted for sport and food. Among the game birds are several species of partridges, pheasants, and quail. The Baluch of the marshy Sistan region between Afghanistan and Iran hunt and fish from reed or dugout boats. They snare birds with the same nets used for fishing. Frogs, toads, and lizards are found in the highlands—including the monitor, which grows to a length of 6 feet (1.8 meters). Among the snakes are some that are highly poisonous—including cobras and several vipers.

Trout, carp, and catfish are among the fish found in the rivers and streams. The largest is a form of European catfish, the *laka*, which can grow to more than 7 feet (2 meters). Many of the insects play important roles as pollinators or biological controls in gardens and fields, but many others spread disease, attack crops, or cause annoyance. Mosquitoes, flies, and biting gnats are found throughout the highlands. Fleas, ticks, lice, and roaches are found, as well. Insect-borne diseases, including malaria and diarrhea, are becoming increasingly widespread.

CHAPTER 4

The Cradle of Civilization

The historical geography of North Africa and the Middle East is very long and extremely complex. As the Cradle of Western Civilization, it also plays a prominent role in our own history. Because of the region's historical importance, its historical geography is divided into two chapters. This chapter focuses on ancient history, whereas the following chapter emphasizes historical developments after the emergence of high civilizations in the eastern Mediterranean region. The arbitrarily selected division point is the dawn of the Christian era.

PREHISTORY

Few regions of the world have had a longer or more continuous period of occupation by the human race's early ancestors. The recent discovery of *Sahelanthropus tchadensis* in the Chadian Sahara documents the presence of relatively advanced hominids in northern Africa 7 million years ago. This would place our ancestors in the region substantially earlier than the better known discoveries in eastern and southern Africa. During this time, North Africa and the Middle East enjoyed tropical and subtropical climates. Even as temperatures cooled during the subsequent Pleistocene (ice age), early man remained established in the region.

Early forms of hominids evolved into the various races of *Homo erectus* some 2 million years ago. The progressively larger and more substantial dwellings found suggest increasingly complex social systems. Settlements tended to be in the same open environments favored by the wild animals on which the hunters depended. Some communities, however, were established in wooded areas near water sources. There, hunters could ambush animals as they were drawn to water and also draw their own domestic water supply. Early simple chopping tools eventually gave way to the more versatile tools of the Acheulian hand-axe culture. The long human evolutionary journey continued with the early use of controlled fire. Hunting techniques became more communal and more sophisticated. Elephants and other game animals were driven into swamps, possibly with the use of fire, thus reducing their mobility and making kills less difficult. Bolas (stones attached to hide ropes and thrown to wrap around the legs of prey) may have been used to immobilize game animals. Such stones have been found in Acheulian encampments. It is assumed that wild vegetable foods, such as nuts, berries, fruits, and roots, would have been exploited as well, but the evidence of their use is seldom preserved in the early sites.

Homo erectus populations evolved into several species and subspecies of the genus *Homo* (meaning human), including the important Neanderthal Man. Neanderthals emerged during the early Upper Pleistocene—approximately 230,000 B.P. (years before the present). Neanderthal males stood about

5 feet 6 inches (1.65 meters) in height. Their cranial capacity was roughly 10 percent greater than that of modern humans. Skeletal evidence from Kebara Cave in Israel suggests that Neanderthals possessed some form of spoken language. They manufactured the broad array of specialized tools associated with the Mousterian culture. In addition, they constructed complex shelters and performed ritual burials, and evidence from Iraq suggests that they used herbal medicines. In North Africa and the Middle East, Neanderthals and fully modern human populations (*Homo sapiens sapiens*) overlapped for a period of roughly 61,000 years. Eventually, around 29,000 years ago, the Neanderthal cultures began to disappear. The more specialized Aterian culture persisted in North Africa. It is credited with the invention of the bow and arrow, which greatly increased effectiveness in hunting. Among the many animals hunted were Barbary sheep, boars, and gazelles.

PLANT AND ANIMAL DOMESTICATION

For more than 90 percent of humankind's estimated 2-million-year history, we have lived as hunters and gatherers. Earliest evidence of domesticated plants and animals appears from about 18,500 years ago, in the Nile Valley. There, the first farmers raised crops that included lentils and chickpeas, primitive forms of wheat and barley, and dates. These crops were eventually followed by beans, grapes, olives, and a broad range of other crops, including beets, carrots, garlic, onions, celery, lettuce, melons, oil seeds, hemp, oats, and rye. By 12,000 years ago, sheep and goats had joined the dog as domesticated animals. Cattle were domesticated around 8,000 B.P., followed by the horse (6,000 B.P.), and later the donkey and camel. By 11,000 B.P., agricultural settlements had emerged in several locations. Evidence points to the existence of ancient agricultural settlements in what is now the basin of the Black Sea. These villages were suddenly displaced when Ice-Age glaciers melted and sea levels rose, flooding the basin and creating the sea around 7,500 B.P.

Hunting and gathering is an efficient form of livelihood requiring little commitment of labor in areas of adequate biological diversity. It is unclear, therefore, why some societies pursued a sedentary agricultural livelihood. In emergent agricultural communities, workload increased and longevity decreased. Indeed, as reflected in the biblical book of Genesis (Chapter 3) agriculture was regarded by some as a curse—a view still held by many pastoral societies. Many factors may have contributed to this view. It is probable that population growth, climate change, and measures to increase the availability of favored plants played a role. In the case of animal domestication, there may have been a scarcity of preferred game animals, or possibly religious or other values were attached to particular species. Claiming orphaned animals as pets is suggested as one contributor to domestication.

As noted elsewhere, the drylands of North Africa and the Middle East were surprisingly fragile. The impact of grazing domesticated livestock contributed to their dramatic transformation. Early written accounts, such as the third-millennium-B.C. Sumerian epic *Gilgamesh*, and modern scientific research support the conclusion that the region's drylands were much more biologically diverse and heavily vegetated at that time than they are today. As grazing lands became less productive, reliance on agriculture increased, and with agriculture came increased social complexity. Sedentary life was also encouraged and reinforced by the emergence of architectural traditions, pottery-making, and other innovations that would have been impractical in pastoral societies. The so-called Urban Revolution was essentially a product of the Agricultural Revolution (or "Neolithic Revolution").

URBAN LIVING

Reference to "revolutions" suggests abrupt widespread change, whereas, in fact, the Agricultural Revolution took place over thousands of years. There are still hunting-and-gathering societies that have not adopted agriculture. Some groups adopted agriculture but later abandoned it to return to hunting and gathering. To many, the emergence of cities is associated with the rise of civilization. Indeed both the terms *city* and *civilization* are derived from the same Latin terms, *civitat, civitas*. Urban life is believed by many to represent social progress. Societies of hunters and gatherers, subsistence farmers, or pastoral nomads are often believed to be remnants of a more primitive past. In fact, particularly within biologically diverse drylands, hunting and gathering and pastoral nomadism are better adapted, more stable forms of livelihood.

By contrast, urban systems often arose in response to the breakdown of more adaptive systems caused by environmental change, external threat, or other factors. Because of the complex webs of dependency that characterize urban civilization, they often fail at some point. We then speak of the rise and fall of urban civilizations. In North Africa and the Middle East, it is not unusual to find the ruins of ancient civilizations providing temporary shelter for pastoral nomads and their flocks as they range over the lands once held by powerful kings or emperors. Similarly, it is not unusual to find cities, such as Damascus, that have prospered for millennia. Urban systems, particularly those that perform beneficial regional functions, are often capable of adapting to changing circumstances. North Africa and the Middle East remains a rich mosaic of ethnic groups and systems of livelihood.

The Sarasvati Valley

Scientists recently discovered a large area of geometrical structures at a depth of 120 feet (36 meters) in northwestern India's Gulf of Khambhat. Further analysis revealed a settlement about 5 miles (8 kilometers) long and 2 miles (3.2 kilometers) wide. Articles later recovered from the site included construction material, sections of walls, pottery, sculpture, beads, and human bones and teeth believed to be roughly 9,500 years old. Although the discovery remains controversial, it should not be surprising. Similar underwater discoveries have been made on the beds of the Black and Mediterranean seas. Early settlements of significant size were typically established along rivers and coastal areas that offered a stable supply of food. During the ice age, huge continental glaciers grew and sea levels fell, thus exposing the sea floor bordering the continents and the beds of shallow seas. As glaciers melted and sea levels rose, many of these settlements disappeared below the rising waters. Because the dates of sea-level rise are relatively well known, such settlements can be assigned to the end of the ice age. This is thousands of years earlier than the first towns and cities of Mesopotamia.

It is obvious that North Africa and the Middle East was not isolated from other areas of the ancient world. In fact, many of its defining traits, such as the Islamic religion, emerged in the relatively recent past. Indeed, the more we learn about prehistoric cultures elsewhere, the more it becomes apparent that a great deal of cultural interaction and exchange took place between this and other, quite distant, regions. North Africa and the Middle East was not an "island" isolated from other places and peoples occupying the Afro-Eurasian landmass. In fact, it benefited greatly from exchanges far and wide.

Mesopotamia

Although urban settlements might first have arisen farther to the east, in present-day India and Pakistan, the processes leading to urbanization are better understood from Mesopotamia. During the fourth millennium B.C., agricultural villages expanded throughout this fertile land between the Tigris and Euphrates rivers. The Ubaid culture was responsible for building the region's first known ziggurats. These temples suggest social stratification. In a stratified society, priests were needed to serve as intermediaries between the people and gods who could either grant abundant harvests or cause disasters if not appeased. This contributed to the emergence of the earliest organized religions.

Located 75 miles south of Baghdad, Iraq, the ziggurat (temple) at Borsippa was excavated in 1980 and is perhaps the best preserved of its kind. The town of Borsippa was located on the east bank of the Euphrates River and was an important religious center in ancient Mesopotamia.

In Mesopotamian antiquity, temples were typically located through geomancy—interpreting natural signs. There was a widespread belief that a shaft, the *axis mundi* (axis of the world), connected the heavens, the earth's surface, and the underworld. The point at which the shaft was believed to pass through the earth's surface was considered to be sacred space. Here was an appropriate place to erect a temple. A flood, an epidemic, a famine, or other disaster could signal the movement of the shaft. A priest or geomancer would be called upon to determine where the shaft now passed through the earth's surface. Based upon his judgment, new temples would be constructed and new communities established around them.

In southern Mesopotamia, it is known that Sumerians constructed irrigation canals to compensate for low rainfall. These early canals assured an agricultural surplus sufficient to support the priests and other specialists not involved in raising crops. As noted in the Bible, the presence of nonagricultural specialists is an essential feature of cities. Construction and management of the canals required strong leadership and a large workforce. This combination of factors resulted in the emergence of cities around 3500 B.C. Although the ruins of these cities lie some distance from any river, the cities were originally established on the banks of the Euphrates—a river that subsequently changed its course.

It is believed that the management of agricultural surpluses and emerging trade among cities led to the development of writing in Sumer. Initially, pictographs of familiar objects were used. Later, the more abstract wedge-shaped characters referred to as cuneiform were inscribed on clay tablets. Among the many other inventions of the Sumerians were the wheel (initially used by potters) and bronze—an alloy of copper and tin. By the twenty-eighth century B.C., writing had spread westward to Egypt and eastward to Elam and the Harappan civilization in the Indus Valley.

Priests shared authority with the leaders of prominent families, who formed councils of elders. In times of need, a chief was appointed. Some believe that as city-states increased in number, competition for land, water, food, guild specialists, and trade increased, as well. Such competition often also led to conflict. Those leaders who were successful in achieving victory in the conflicts remained in power and became kings. The kings increased their control by building palaces near the temples. This made it possible for them to combine their authority with that of the priests and the gods the priests controlled. These changing relationships are reflected in royal burials dating from around 2500 B.C. The kings evidently saw themselves as being godlike, and looked forward to a comfortable afterlife. Buried with the kings were palace retainers and objects that had supported or entertained them in life—such as chariots, boats, game boards, musical instruments, and jewelry. Among the most prominent Mesopotamian city-states were Ur and Uruk. Surrounded by protective walls of mud brick, Ur had an estimated population of 30,000 people, and Uruk is believed to have been home to more than 50,000.

Mesopotamian societies became highly stratified, and an enormous gap divided rich and poor. Rulers and their associates controlled considerable wealth. Somewhat less powerful were the guilds and other associations upon which the aristocracy depended. These included specialists such as scribes, architects and builders, metallurgists, merchants, and bakers and brewers. These groups were typically unrelated to the aristocracy. Rather, they were often bound to their masters by negotiated agreements or guarantees of protection. If dissatisfied, they could accept patronage elsewhere, thus impoverishing a city-state or kingdom. Therefore, the ability of city-states, kingdoms, and empires of antiquity to attract and retain important guilds was a key to their survival and prosperity. On the lower rungs of the social ladder were slaves, individuals who had fallen from grace, were in debt, or who "came with the land."

In Sumer, writing made it possible for legal systems to become formally established. These systems, in turn, assured individuals of certain rights. Guilds were attached to the aristocracy through mutual agreement and contracts. The legal systems also permitted some upward social mobility. For example, if a slave married a free person, their children would be free. Women enjoyed a range of rights, including the ownership of property, but could be divorced if they failed to bear children.

In 2334 B.C., Sumer, weakened by conflict, fell to the armies of Sargon of Akkad—a land to the north of Sumer. Sargon unified the city-states of Mesopotamia, creating the first known empire. His empire extended from the Zagros Mountains and the Persian Gulf to the Mediterranean Sea. Akkadian, a Semitic language, became the *lingua franca* (commonly used language) of the realm. About 135 years later, Akkad fell into disarray, and anarchy prevailed throughout the region.

From the chaos, Sumerians again gained control and established a united Sumer and Akkad, with its capital at Ur. Active trade relationships were established with Dilmun on the Persian Gulf, as well with the Harappan civilization of the Indus River valley.

PATTERNS OF CHANGE

By the fifth millennium B.C., agriculture had spread throughout much of North Africa and the Middle East, copper had acquired importance in the manufacture of tools and implements, and pottery came into use throughout the region. Many of the changes that took place suggest the emergence of more sedentary livelihood systems. Large-scale migrations changed the ethnic and linguistic composition of the region. The growing ethnic complexity is reflected in Egyptian history. Although Egypt is often thought to be an isolated, ethnically unified kingdom, nothing could be further from the truth. At various times, it was governed by Nubians, Libyans, the Hyksos, Ethiopians, Assyrians, Persians, Greeks, and Romans, as well as a host of others in the more recent past. In fact, Egyptians spent more time under foreign domination than under their own native leaders. Egypt's ethnic diversity is further emphasized by a historical reference to there being 70 languages spoken within the kingdom.

Early Egypt

Partially in contrast with Mesopotamia, Egypt witnessed a lengthy period of development with quite different patterns of settlement and ecological adaptation. It had a long history of plant and animal domestication, irrigated agriculture, village settlement, and many temples and tombs. Despite these characteristics, Egypt developed little of the social complexity of Mesopotamia and remained essentially rural in character. Only Memphis and Luxor-Karnak qualified as urban centers. As was true of the North African and Middle Eastern drylands in general, Egypt witnessed dramatic environmental change. Prior to the third millennium B.C., the region's climate had been considerably more moist. As it became increasingly arid, however, many animals began to disappear. Elephants, rhinoceroses, giraffes, and many other species disappeared altogether from northern Egypt. Lions, leopards, and Barbary sheep became uncommon, as wooded savannahs gave way to increasingly parched desert conditions. They were gradually replaced by species that were better adapted to desert environments.

Changing environmental conditions were brought about by factors other than climate change. Livestock grazing, agricultural expansion, and the ever-increasing need for wood as fuel and building material also resulted in massive changes in natural vegetation. The changing wildlife composition of Egypt reflected both habitat loss and increased hunting pressure. Drying conditions increased Egypt's dependence on the waters of the Nile River. In fact, large flat-bottomed basins for growing crops were excavated along the river banks. The basins were equipped with simple sluices, devices that diverted water into them during the peak of the annual flood. These changes prompted Herodotus to comment that one "… can easily see that the Egypt to which the Greeks sail is new land which the Egyptians have gained as a gift from the river." On the floodplain of the Nile, patterns of settlement and systems of livelihood were both affected by the extent and considerable variability of the Nile floods.

Almost all pyramids built during the Age of the Pyramids (2780–2258 B.C.) were located on the fringe of the desert, west of the Nile near Memphis. The ground on which they were constructed is said to have been reclaimed from the river by the pharaoh Menes. Although the pyramids of Giza are particularly well known, there are more than 80 of the structures scattered along the Nile. They evolved from simple covered pit burials (*mastabas*), through a variety of step pyramids, to the massive true pyramids dating from the Fourth Dynasty (2575–2465 B.C.).

The selection of a pyramid construction site was of particular importance. Several factors had to be considered: It had to be situated west of the river—the side of the setting sun. It was to stand well above the level of the river, but not be too remote from its west bank. The geological structure upon which it was built was to be free from defects or a tendency to crack. It was to be situated close to the capital and to a residence of the king. The motive for investing such time and effort in the building of a tomb was the belief that gaining a desired afterlife was dependent upon two primary conditions: The body must be preserved from disturbance or destruction, and the material needs of both the deceased and his *ka* must be supplied. (The ka is sometimes believed to be a twin or double of the deceased, and sometimes an embodiment of the life force, a protective spirit, a personification of abstract qualities essential for a continuance of this life, or some combination of concepts.) The Great Pyramid of Giza, the tomb of Khufu, is the oldest of the Seven Wonders of the Ancient World. (The remaining six wonders are also located in North Africa, the eastern Mediterranean Basin, and the Middle East: the

The Pyramids of Giza, near Cairo, Egypt, were built during the Fourth Dynasty (2575–2465 B.C.) on the west bank of the Nile River. The Great Pyramid of Giza (right) is the largest of these pyramids and was constructed as a tomb for the Egyptian pharaoh Khufu.

Hanging Gardens of Babylon; the Statue of Zeus at Olympia; the Temple of Artemis at Ephesus; the Mausoleum at Halicarnassus; the Colossus of Rhodes; and the Lighthouse of Alexandria.)

THE THIRD MILLENNIUM B.C.

Beyond Mesopotamia and Egypt, the third millennium witnessed continued cultural change. Other civilizations emerged at the doorstep of North Africa and the Middle East. To the west, on the island of Crete in the eastern Mediterranean, the advanced Minoan civilization thrived. Eastward, in the Indus Valley, the Harappan civilization grew around the cities of

Mohenjo-daro and Harappa. Both the Minoan and Harappan civilizations were important to North Africa and the Middle East. For one reason, they engaged in active trade. The Minoan trade network included linkages to Cyprus, Anatolia, Syria, Egypt, and Mesopotamia. They traded tin and copper (the components of bronze), gold and silver, ceramics, and saffron (a spice). Harappan cities traded with Mesopotamia, the Persian Gulf, and other distant lands. Among the goods they exported were cotton, spices, ivory, precious stones, and jewelry. A continued mixing of peoples also took place as different groups migrated into the region from elsewhere. Through the process of diffusion, new ideas and material goods continued to enrich the region's culture.

Elsewhere, powerful tribes of Berbers gained strength in North Africa. Eventually, they ruled Egypt for a time and also played an important role in the development of Carthage. The state of Kush was rising to prominence in the southern borderlands of Egypt. The Hittites emerged from the Aegean region around 2250 B.C. and expanded eastward into Anatolia. There, they encountered the Hattic people, who were engaged in highly sophisticated metallurgy. The origin of Hattic metallurgy is unknown, but it dates from at least 2500 B.C. As the Hittites established themselves in Anatolia, Iranians entered the Middle East from the steppes of Central Asia.

THE SECOND MILLENNIUM B.C.

The Second Millennium B.C. saw the emergence of several very important civilizations. It was also a period of continued cultural change and periodic conflict between competing empires.

Hittites

Hittites were a warlike people who differed greatly from the peaceful Minoans. Beginning in the seventeenth century B.C., their empire began to spread throughout central Anatolia, from where they conducted many raids southward into

Mesopotamia. By perhaps 1400 B.C., the Hittites had become actively engaged in iron working. With their weapons of iron, as well as their highly maneuverable horse-drawn war chariots, they held a decided military advantage. In fact, they were frequently engaged in military campaigns against such powerful rival kingdoms as Egypt, Babylonia, and Assyria.

Hittite governance was dominated by a king, who also served as the supreme priest, military commander, and chief judge. Many laws and customs were borrowed from the Babylonians. Their art and architecture were similarly influenced by their neighbors. The Hittite economy was based on agriculture. Livestock chiefly included cattle and sheep. As with other Indo-European-speaking peoples, cattle enjoyed a special status. Barley and wheat were the chief crops. Although the Hittites possessed reserves of copper, iron, silver, and lead, they did not engage actively in trade with their neighbors. The possession of metals, after all, gave them a powerful military advantage that they were unwilling to share with others. As with other kingdoms in North Africa and the Middle East, guilds or guild-like associations were active in the Hittite kingdoms. Particularly noteworthy was the guild of Hattic metallurgists. As Hittite authority waned in the face of more powerful opponents around 1200 B.C., the guilds of metallurgists sought security elsewhere. Their dispersal throughout North Africa and the Middle East ushered in the Iron Age.

The Hyksos

The seventeenth century B.C. was one of considerable upheaval. Various migrations resulted in widespread social displacement and political realignment throughout much of the region. The Hyksos rose to prominence in the Nile Delta around 1674 B.C. and ruled Lower and Middle Egypt for more than a century. Somewhat surprisingly, little is known of their origin or identity. Like the Hittites, the Hyksos entered battle in horse-drawn chariots, rather than the more traditional four-wheeled wagons drawn by onagers (donkey-like animals).

Further, their military hardware included the powerful bow, improved arrowheads, and a variety of swords and daggers. For self-protection, they also had a new type of shield, protective shirts, and metal helmets.

Despite their greater mobility and superior weapons, there is little evidence of an armed invasion of Egypt by the Hyksos. It is now believed that they may simply have migrated into the Nile Delta, and that the Egyptian rulers were too inept, intimidated, or busy with internal problems to stem the migration. The Hyksos brought political stability to Egypt, but were understandably resented by the native aristocracy. They were driven from Egypt around 1550 B.C. In Egyptian literature, "Hyksos" remained a synonym for "Asiatic," and was often applied to non-Egyptian groups such as the Habiru. This might have led the Egyptians to relate the arrival of the Hyksos with the Egyptian travels of Joseph and his brothers. As a result, many modern historians identify the expulsion of the Hyksos with the Exodus. In fact, it was during the later reign of Rameses II (1290–1224 B.C.) that the Habiru slaves revolted and escaped into Gilead, marking the beginning of Jewish history.

As noted earlier, the Minoan civilization was effectively destroyed around 1500 B.C. with the volcanic eruption on the island of Thíra, and the resultant tsunami (tidal wave). This roughly coincides with the fall of the Old Hittite Kingdom and the expulsion of the Hyksos from Egypt.

The Philistines

The Philistines were a minor group that migrated to the Levant (eastern shore of the Mediterranean) from the Aegean Sea area around 1180 B.C. Egyptian literature identifies them as being "Sea People." Because several ethnic groups comprised the Sea People, it is probable that Philistia was ethnically diverse, as well, and that the Philistines were the dominant group. They occupied five cities along the eastern Mediterranean shores. The Philistines apparently welcomed members of the iron-smithing guild displaced with the fall of the Hittites. They long held a monopoly on iron smithing in the Levant. The smiths also worked in silver and bronze. The Philistines were further known for the quality of their agriculture, for the introduction of new crops, and for their wine and olive oil. They were also actively engaged in trade. The Philistines eventually lost their independence around 736 B.C. and later came under the control of many different empires. Historically and culturally, their chief importance is that they, together with several other local ethnic groups, were ancestors to the modern Palestinian Arabs.

THE FIRST MILLENNIUM B.C.

Around 1000 B.C., the Philistines' dominance in the Levant was broken by the neighboring Phoenicians and Hebrews. Phoenicians replaced the Philistines as the prominent maritime power in the eastern Mediterranean. Led by the city-state of Tyre, the Phoenicians expanded trade westward to the mineral-rich Iberian Peninsula. Of particular interest were gold and silver, as well as tin and copper for the manufacture of brass. The Phoenicians were well known for their skill in shipbuilding. They also were skilled in building with wood and stone, metal working, pottery and textile making, and creating the purple dye derived from the murex shell. They were well known for their jewelers, works of art, and agriculture. Barley and other grains were of importance, as were wine, olives, figs, and the date-palm.

To the east, a resurgent Assyria consolidated its control over northern Mesopotamia and reduced Babylonia to weakened dependency. In Anatolia, a challenge to Assyrian dominance rose in the form of Urartu (Ararat)—a remarkable kingdom led by a Caucasian-speaking elite. As history remembers Assyria for its aggressive behavior, Urartu is remembered for its apparent gender equality, its sophisticated art and metal work, bronze figurines, as well as its remarkable architectural

Much of the present-day Middle East was united under Assyrian rule from the eighth to the seventh century B.C. Although known for their aggressive behavior, the Assyrians weren't solely conquerors; they also were prodigious builders, constructing palaces such as this one at Nimrud.

and engineering accomplishments. The latter included multistoried buildings, subterranean aqueducts, and remarkable inverted siphons that carried water across valleys through underground channels.

The Assyrian expansion late in the ninth century B.C. weakened several kingdoms and dispersed the ruling elite and their attendant guilds. The Assyrian expansion was inadvertently aided by the pressure exerted by pastoral nomads on the northern frontier of the Middle East. Seeking refuge, many exiled elites established kingdoms beyond the reach of the Assyrians. With these migrations, iron working and other guild specialties expanded greatly in North Africa and the Middle East, as did the trade networks that served the region. Indeed, the Phoenicians and other merchants almost certainly traveled well beyond the Mediterranean for resources and trade. Some scholars believe that they even reached the shores of the Americas two millennia before the documented European Voyages of Discovery.

Media, their Iranian allies, Babylonia, and Urartu combined their forces to overwhelm Assyria around 610 B.C. At roughly the same time, perhaps in response to social unrest, Zoroastrianism and Buddhism arose on the eastern frontiers of the Middle East. In Egypt, Pharaoh Necho II sponsored a circumnavigation of Africa undertaken by Phoenician navigators. Later, in 559 B.C., Cyrus II (Cyrus the Great) initiated a series of conquests that resulted in the expansion of the Persian Empire from Central Asia to Libya and Macedonia in the west. The Achaemenid rulers governed with a light hand, and the region prospered.

The principal changes during the fourth century B.C. included the weakening of the Achaemenid Empire and its withdrawal from Egypt, the Aegean, and the Indus Valley. From its hearth in North Africa, Carthage expanded northward into Sicily and westward to the Iberian Peninsula. The Carthaginians established colonies beyond the Pillars of Heracles (the Strait of Gibraltar), along Africa's northwest coast, and on several islands in the Atlantic Ocean. Trade expanded further, as tin from Britain's Cornwall Peninsula, amber from the shores of the Baltic Sea, and ivory from India and Africa were brought back to Carthage. Many other commodities from distant lands also found their way into the marketplaces of North Africa and the Middle East. As trade flourished, the Lydians introduced the use of gold and silver coins and, according to Greek geographer and historian Herodotus, were the first to sell goods by retail. With expanded commerce and the need for record keeping came a substantial fourth-century expansion of literacy.

One of history's greatest territorial conquests was that conducted under the leadership of Alexander ("The Great") of Macedonia. Alexander's empire ultimately included much of the world as known by eastern Mediterranean peoples. It stretched from the Balkan Peninsula and Egypt in the west, eastward into Central Asia and western India. Alexander died before his empire was politically consolidated.

The third century B.C. witnessed the decline of Carthage and the rise of the kingdoms of Mauritania and Numidia in North Africa. Elsewhere, many kingdoms fragmented as others rose. By 100 B.C., Rome had absorbed the Carthaginian and Ptolemaic (Egyptian) lands of North Africa. The Romans were prevented from expanding eastward by several Semitic kingdoms. Farther to the north was an expanding Armenian Empire. Farther to the east was the increasingly formidable Parthian Empire and the Eastern Iranian principalities. As the millennium ended, Rome controlled the kingdoms of North Africa, the Levant, and most of Anatolia. Armenia continued to control eastern Anatolia, and the powerful Parthian Empire prevented Roman expansion into eastern Syria and Mesopotamia. Clearly, the center of power had shifted westward to Mediterranean Europe. This change in events is a logical breaking point in the historical geography of North Africa and the Middle East.

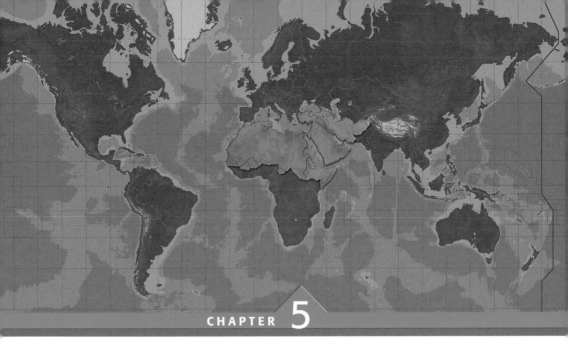

Western Influence

By the dawn of the Christian era, the winds of change began to blow across North Africa and the Middle East. The center of cultural influence and power had shifted westward, to Greece and then to Rome. Although lying outside the region, these European centers had a profound influence on events in North Africa and the Middle East. This chapter details the key events of the region's historical geography during the past two millennia.

THE FIRST MILLENNIUM A.D.
During the first century A.D., the balance of power within the region changed little. Roman influence and control remained widespread. Nevertheless, Roman rule was increasingly challenged in the Middle

East, as indicated by the Jewish Revolt of A.D. 66. During the early centuries of the millennium, trade continued to thrive throughout much of the region. Despite various political divisions, trade expanded within both the Middle East and North Africa, including eastward, over what was to become the famous Silk Road into China.

By the dawn of the fifth century A.D., the Roman Empire was divided into western and eastern realms. Huns, fierce nomadic warriors from Central Asia, became a rising power on the northern frontier of the Eastern Roman Empire. By the midpoint of the millennium, the Vandal Kingdom arose in former Carthaginian territory, and in northwestern Africa, there was growing Berber resistance to Roman rule. During the sixth century, the Eastern Roman Empire, under Emperor Justinian, reclaimed much of the western Mediterranean that had fallen to the Vandals, Berbers, and others. The empire was beginning to fray on the edges, particularly in the east. Turkish tribes were rising to prominence, and Persians reclaimed Egypt and the Levant. By the mid-seventh century, the Eastern Roman Empire (now known as the Byzantine Empire) and the Sasanian (Persian) Empire faced a new challenge—the rise of Islam. The Arabs, spiritually and politically united by Muhammad ibn Abdullah, were poised to transform much of the Middle East, North Africa, and beyond.

Medieval History

The Prophet Muhammad was born around A.D. 570. He was a member of the Hashim Clan of the Quraysh Tribe, and was raised in a leading family in Mecca, which at the time was a large, highly civilized center of trade and commerce. The stature of Mecca was particularly enhanced by the presence of two significant features: the Well of Zamzam, which made Mecca a regionally important source of water on the coastal trade route, and the *Ka'ba* (Kaabah), an ancient shrine that housed idols and the Black Stone of Mecca—a meteorite. As a center of trade,

The town of Mecca, in present-day Saudi Arabia, was a center of commerce and trade around the time of the Prophet Muhammad's birth in A.D. 570. As Islam spread throughout the Middle East, Mecca also became an important religious center. Pictured here is Mecca's Great Mosque, which is considered the most sacred Muslim shrine.

Mecca was also a center of intellectual exchange. Muhammad spent most of his life engaged in trade, meditation, preaching, lawgiving, and organizing. His creed of Islam was adopted by almost all of the inhabitants of Mecca and Medina, because of its appealing content and Muhammad's sincerity.

The name *Islam* means "submission to the will of Allah." It reflected the sayings of Muhammad, the culture and environment of the Arabian Peninsula, and elements of Judaism and Christianity. In preaching his revelations, Muhammad denounced the idols of the Ka'ba. Local resistance to his teachings resulted in the flight of Muhammad and his followers to a city some 210 miles (340 kilometers) north of Mecca, Al Madina

Al Munawwara, or present-day Medina. The year of the flight (*Hegira*), A.D. 622, marks the first year of the Islamic calendar. Muslim years are based on the 29.5-day lunar cycle, which makes them 11 days shorter than years established using the solar Gregorian calendar.

Unlike Judaism, an *ethnic* religion that does not seek converts, Islam was a *proselytizing* religion that enjoyed wide appeal. The spread of Islam occurred rapidly. Within two years of Muhammad's death, Arabia was reunited and devout adherents to the faith had been dispatched to Egypt, Syria, and Mesopotamia. By midcentury, the Muslim Arabs had extended their influence from Tripoli (in present-day northwestern Libya) into Central Asia. Signs of disagreement among Muslims emerged upon the death of the third caliph (successor of Muhammad as the head of Islam), Uthman, who held the leadership position from 644 to 656. After his death, Muhammad's son-in-law Ali became caliph. The Umayyad Dynasty, which was not closely related to Muhammad, regained the caliphate upon Ali's death. For many Muslims, there was both opposition to Umayyad rule and to the belief that Ali and his descendants were the rightful heirs of the Prophet. This led to the principal division within Islam, that between Orthodox (Sunni) and Alid (Shi'ite) Islam. The division was occasionally seized by the heirs of earlier empires and kingdoms, such as those of Persia and Yemen, to accept Islam in the form of Shi'ism, while rejecting a foreign orthodoxy.

In the eighth century, a reenergized Umayyad Caliphate began a period of rapid expansion. It expanded westward across North Africa to the Atlantic Ocean. By the early eighth century, its influence had spread northward into the Iberian Peninsula and southern France. Eastward, the caliphate consolidated its authority in Central Asia and the Indus River valley. Islam, at least for a time, had brought peace and unity to an area as extensive as the Roman Empire. In addition, trade, the arts, and science flourished with the active support of the caliphate. In 749, the Umayyad Dynasty was overthrown by the Abbasids, who, although supported by the Shi'ites, opted for orthodoxy. The Umayyads had governed from Damascus, but the Abbasids founded a new capital, Baghdad (in present-day Iraq). Under Caliph Harun al-Rashid, Baghdad became the most productive cultural center in the medieval world. In the ninth century, the margins of the Abbasid Caliphate were lost to Islamic competitors—including newly established Shi'ite caliphates. Perhaps most unexpected was the rise of the Shi'ite Qarmatians in Arabia.

A.D. 1000 TO 1500

The dawn of the second millennium witnessed the growing strength and importance of the Turks. Particularly noteworthy was the rise of the Ghaznavid Emirate, which became an important center of religion, literature, and science during the reign of Yamin ad-Dawlah Mahmud. Mahmud was a patron of the arts and literature and was said to have had 900 resident scholars, including the scientist-historian Al-Biruni and the poet Firdousi, in his House of Learning. The Turkish presence further increased with the arrival of the Seljuks, nomadic warriors from Central Asia. Their authority extended from their Central Asian homeland to Anatolia, the eastern Mediterranean Sea, and southward to the holy places of Arabia.

The eleventh century witnessed the first of the Christian crusades, launched to free Jerusalem and the Holy Land from Muslim rule. These attempts lasted several centuries and involved many (nine major and several minor) different groups of crusaders from various areas of Western Europe. Meanwhile, the Muslim foothold in the Iberian Peninsula gradually gave way to the advances of Christian kingdoms of Portugal, and the Spanish centers focusing upon Leon, Castile, Navarre, and Aragon. Further disruption came from the east. Military campaigns led by the powerful Mongol chieftain Genghis Khan (Temujin) and his successors began transforming the Middle

East. The Mongols had created a vast empire that extended from Korea to Persia. Plans to further extend the empire westward into Europe were abandoned in the mid-thirteenth century, when the khan died.

The fourteenth century was a period of considerable turbulence and disruption in the region. In the Iberian Peninsula, the Islamic presence was reduced to the Emirate of Granada, located in southern Spain, south of the Guadalquivir River. The Mamluk Sultanate continued to dominate Egypt and the Levant. In Anatolia and the Caucasus Mountains region, continued fragmentation occurred, resulting in scores of principalities, sultanates, emirates, and empires. The most important of these was the Ottoman Sultanate. At roughly the same time, in 1346, the Black Death (bubonic plague) spread into the region from Central Asia, causing further disruption.

By the dawn of the fifteenth century, the political map of North Africa and the Middle East was somewhat simplified. North Africa was dominated by sultanates or caliphates in Morocco in the west, Tunisia in the center, and Egypt in the east. The Ottoman Sultanate consolidated its authority in Anatolia. A single emirate held control over Mesopotamia, Iran, and the lands to the east. The medieval period was one of great change in North Africa and the Middle East. Islam and Christianity clashed; migrants entered the region bringing new languages and ethnicities, and often conflict; economic fortunes rose in some areas and fell in others; and empires and caliphates underwent great change as alliances fragmented or pulled together as political units through time.

During most of the medieval period, very few important developments occurred in science and technology. Toward the end of the period, however, several major innovations appeared that literally altered the course of history. The magnetic compass, gunpowder, and printing all entered the region, perhaps from China. These and other innovations led to advances in navigation, mining and metallurgy, and manufacturing.

Scientists began to ask new questions and addressed new issues, greatly expanding knowledge.

MODERN HISTORY

It may seem strange to refer to a time period beginning 500 years ago as "Modern History," but in many respects, this is the case. Political, economic, and numerous other events of the past half-millennium have combined to create today's North Africa and Middle East.

The Ottomans, like the Seljuks, were a Turkish tribe that converted to Islam before migrating onto the plateaus of Iran and Anatolia. They steadily expanded from a foothold in northern Anatolia to forge a vast empire. Eventually, the Ottomans controlled a territory extending from Europe's Danube River to the southern tip of the Arabian Peninsula, and including vast areas of northern Africa. It is said that as pastoral nomads, the Ottomans administered people and territory in much the same way they herded livestock. As nomads, they separated types of livestock from one another, grazing each within its own territory. As rulers, the Ottomans made no attempt to create a single, unified state. Rather, they allowed differences of race, religion, ethnicity, and general outlook to continue. The extent of the empire remained relatively constant from 1566 until the end of World War I. In fact, a single dynasty had held the Ottoman Sultanate for some 600 years—a remarkable accomplishment in this turbulent region.

In Persia, a group known as Safavids emerged on the plateau of Iran around 1500. Unlike the relatively stable Ottomans, Persians progressed through a succession of dynasties. During this period, Persia (present-day Iran) occasionally contended with the Ottomans for authority in Mesopotamia, but they failed to greatly expand their territory beyond its original stronghold. Thus, from the end of the medieval period to World War I, North Africa and the Middle East was home to two dominant powers. The powerful and expansionist

Ottoman Empire was based in Anatolia, from which it spread over a broad area, and the Persian empires and kingdoms were based on the plateau of Iran.

During the modern period, Europeans and others viewed the region as one of great wealth and mystery. From the nineteenth century onward, commercial and diplomatic ties became well established, linking regional governing elites with European powers. With European colonial expansion, the status of North Africa and the Middle East changed greatly. Centers of power shifted. Much greater emphasis was placed on the actual or potential importance of the region to European objectives, including designs of global dominance. Europe's role in this regard is reflected in the "Heartland" concept developed by British geographer Sir Halford J. Mackinder:

Who rules Eastern Europe commands the Heartland;
Who rules the Heartland commands the World-Island;
Who rules the World-Island commands the World.

A competing concept was developed by Nicholas John Spykman. It foresaw the global dominance of a single superpower through control of "Rimlands" (lands surrounding the Heartland). Spykman believed that whomever controlled the Rimlands would control the Heartland, hence, the World-Island. Basic to both the Heartland and Rimland concepts is the idea of a "World Island" composed of Europe, Asia, and Africa, and focusing on the strategically located Middle East.

As European dominance increased, North Africa and the Middle East became associated with a number of other well-known geopolitical issues. For example, following the end of World War I (1918), the region became divided into political units artificially imposed by European powers. Many of the boundaries were drawn without regard to local institutions, socioeconomic arrangements, or other unifying geographic elements or conditions. By 1943, only seven of the region's principal states were independent—Egypt, Turkey, Iraq, Iran, Saudi Arabia, Oman, and Yemen. Others were created later, or only recently gained their independence. Various organizations, such as the Arab League, were formed in an attempt to coordinate issues of regional political and economic concern. The region has also been linked to more broadly based organizations that were believed to serve the interests of regional governments. For example, several countries are members of the Organization of Petroleum Exporting Countries (OPEC).

Discovery and commercial development of petroleum and natural gas deposits has played a major role in the modern history of the region. The first oil wells appeared in the Caspian basin during the 1870s, just as industrialization began to boom in Europe and North America. Since that time, industrialized states have been deeply involved in the region's political and economic affairs. In some cases, strong ties have been established with local governing elites, such as the Saudi dynasty. In other instances, uncooperative governments, such as that of Iraq in the recent past, have exposed themselves to military retaliation by petroleum-dependent industrialized states.

As noted earlier, management of water resources has been a major issue for the region for many years. Recently, water has become an increasingly volatile concern. On the Nile River, for example, officials from upper basin countries are beginning to discuss the development of irrigation projects that would affect the downstream availability of water in Egypt. A similar problem exists with Turkey's GAP project that threatens the agricultural economies of Syria and Iraq. Water of the Jordan River is sharply declining in both quantity and quality, affecting availability and use in Syria, Jordan, and Israel. Some observers suggest that water will play as important a role in the twenty-first century as did petroleum during the 1900s.

The Arab-Israeli issue continues to plague the region. Persecution of Eastern European Jews in the 1880s led to a movement, *Hovevei Tzion* (Lovers of Zion), or Zionist, which encouraged migration to Palestine. The movement became more highly organized through the efforts of a Hungarian journalist, Theodor Herzl, who, in the late 1890s, called for the creation of an independent state for Jews in Palestine. One Zionist leader, writing in 1901, encouraged immigration for "a people without a land for a land without people." This is one of many essentially colonialist attitudes expressed, showing little regard to the existence and rights of the roughly 400,000 Arabs who then resided in Palestine. The collapse of the Ottoman Empire after World War I presented a new opportunity for political reorganization in the Middle East and the creation of a Jewish sanctuary. This was expressed in the 1917 Balfour Declaration:

> His Majesty's Government views with favour the establishment in Palestine of a national home for the Jewish people, and will use their best endeavours to facilitate the achievement of this object, it being clearly understood that nothing shall be done which may prejudice the civil and religious rights of existing non-Jewish communities in Palestine, or the rights and political status enjoyed by Jews in any other country.

A subsequent 1922 British "White Paper" sought to clarify the contradictory elements of the declaration, assuring the Arab population that Britain fully intended to protect their rights. The brutality of the Holocaust understandably encouraged further immigration. The efforts of Jewish activist organizations further advanced their cause, and Israel became an independent state in 1948. Since that time, the former Palestine and its Palestinian residents have experienced partition, warfare, refugee issues, economic discrimination, and fierce competition for water resources. These and a host of other problems have contributed to the instability of North Africa and the Middle East.

The Iran-Iraq War of 1980–1988 was another defining political event in the region's modern history. Ancient hostilities came to the surface soon after the Iranian Revolution of

In the late 1800s, European Jews, led by Theodor Herzl, established the Zionist movement, which supported the creation of a Jewish state in Palestine. Although it took some 50 years for official recognition, Israel became an independent state in 1948. Pictured here is Israel's prime minister David Ben-Gurion during the proclamation of nationhood in May of that year. Above Ben-Gurion is a painting of Herzl.

1979. To the Iraqi government, Iran's boldness seemed to be matched by the country's vulnerability. Encouraged by what it believed to be Iran's weakness, Iraq made a number of demands that Iran was unwilling to accept, resulting in the onset of war. It was assumed by many that the war would last for only a few weeks. Incredibly, it lasted for eight years and cost more than 500,000 lives. Iraq's economic losses in the war with Iran contributed to the country's decision to invade Kuwait in 1990. As is often the case, Iraq justified its military action as an effort to bring freedom and independence to an oppressed people. The Gulf War of 1990–1991 resulted in the expulsion of Iraq from Kuwait by the United States and its allies and the placing of severe sanctions upon the Iraqi government.

It became apparent to the oil-dependent Western countries that North Africa and the Middle East was becoming increasingly unstable. The region's apparent vulnerability to revolution encouraged the first U.S. Bush administration to link its response to Iraq's invasion of Kuwait to the U.S. "right" of access to petroleum declared under the (U.S. President Jimmy) Carter Doctrine. The Doctrine was originally written in 1980 to deter the Soviets from trying to gain a foothold in the Persian Gulf area. A "War on Terror" was declared by the second Bush administration (and allies) in 2003 in the belief that Iraq represented a mounting threat to global stability.

Strategic interests, including the security of shipping lanes, have resulted in renewed interest in geopolitically significant horns and straits. They include the Strait of Bab el-Mandeb, the Suez Canal, the straits of Bosporus and Dardanelles in Turkey, the Strait of Hormuz, and the Strait of Tiran connecting the Red Sea and the Gulf of Aqaba. These so-called "chokepoints" effectively control the flow of oil to industrial countries in Europe, North America, and the Far East. Hence, their status directly affects the economies of the industrialized world.

The political landscape of North Africa and the Middle East is changing. The Persian monarchy continued until the revolution of 1979. (The name was officially changed from Persia to Iran by the Pahlavis in 1935, and to the Islamic Republic of Iran after the revolution.) According to experts on the region, present-day Turkey, Iran, Egypt, and often-contested Mesopotamia (Iraq) have long been the four principal centers of power in North Africa and the Middle East. Minor cores of power existed in Morocco, Tunisia, Saudi Arabia, Yemen, and Oman. The principal cores have appeared and reappeared as major centers of power throughout history. Anatolia and Iran, from which the most extensive geographical areas have been controlled, are centered in relatively secure plateaus. These centers are home to two of the region's three most populous and powerful states, Turkey and Iran. Both countries have a population of about 70 million and a military exceeding one-half million troops. They are joined by Egypt in both population (estimated at 77 million) and military strength (450,000 troops). Although Mesopotamia (Iraq) was a center of power for 1700 years, it later lost much of its earlier strength and influence.

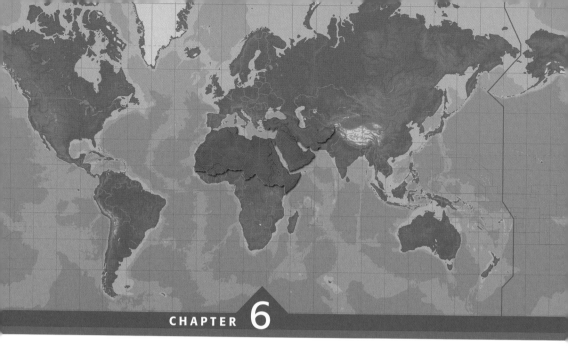

CHAPTER 6

Population
and Settlement

Water is essential to life, and perhaps nowhere else in the world is this better illustrated than in North Africa and the Middle East. The desert core of the Sahara and most arid portions of the Arabian Peninsula occupy an area roughly the size of the United States. Yet these parched landscapes, combined, are home to only a million or so widely scattered people and no railroad or paved highway crosses either area. The "World at Night" image appearing in the front of this book shows these core desert regions to be nearly as blank as the vast oceans. A few specks of light—islands in the oceans and oases in the desert—stand out in a sea of darkness.

The World at Night image also shows the importance of water in a desert region. Just as flakes of metal are drawn to a magnet, people are drawn to reliable sources of fresh water in desert lands. As you learned in previous chapters, oasis sites have long attracted settlements. The world's first cities grew around oases in Southwest Asia. Such early urban centers as Ur, Jarmo, Jericho, and Biblos each developed around life-sustaining sources of fresh water. So did some of the world's leading urban centers, such as Constantinople (present-day Istanbul, Turkey), Baghdad (Iraq), Damascus (Syria), and both Cairo and Alexandria (Egypt).

POPULATION

Census data for much of North Africa and the Middle East tend to be unreliable. Figures often vary greatly. Taking a detailed census, after all, is difficult, costly, and beyond the reach of many poor countries. In the United States, taking a reliable head count every 10 years is required by the Constitution. The number of representatives each state can send to Congress is determined by its population. Having a representative government, however, is not a factor in most countries within the region under discussion. In terms of demographic (population) data, specific figures are of little importance. Does it really matter, for example, whether Egypt has 77.5 million (CIA World Factbook), 76.1 million (U.S. Census Bureau), or 74 million (Population Reference Bureau) people? Our concern is with general conditions, patterns, and trends. For example, it is useful to know whether a region or country ranks higher, lower, or about the same as other places in the world in terms of its demographic conditions. General information about population density, birth and death rates, life expectancy, and other important conditions of the human population is essential to understanding a region's geographic patterns.

Despite the region's environmental limitations, North Africa and the Middle East is home to an estimated 400 million people. Populations range from about 70 million in Egypt, Turkey, and Iran to fewer than one million in Bahrain, Qatar, and Western Sahara. (Readers interested in obtaining specific population

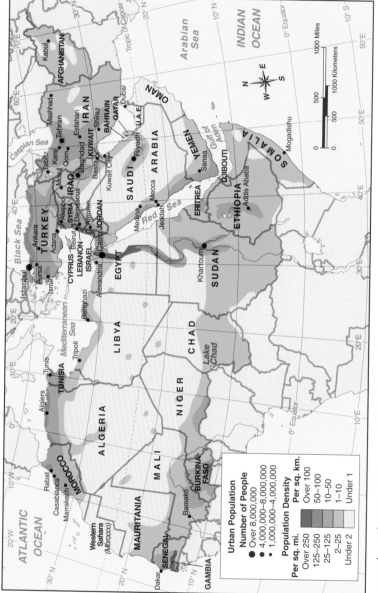

Approximately 400 million people live in North Africa and the Middle East; more than half of whom live in Egypt, Iran, and Turkey. The largest metropolitan areas include Cairo, Egypt (14 million), Tehran, Iran (10.7 million), and Istanbul, Turkey (10.4 million).

data for individual countries are referred to the CIA World Fact-book, or some other reliable source for such information.)

CHARACTERISTICS OF POPULATION GROWTH

Islam, data suggest, is the world's fastest growing faith. How is this phenomenon explained? The answer lies in very high birth-rates and rates of natural increase (RNI) within most North African and Middle Eastern countries. In 2005, the world's RNI dropped to 1.2 percent per year (from an all-time high of 2.0 percent during the 1970s). Today, the rate of natural increase for North Africa is 2.0 percent, identical to the world's all-time high rate of growth. In war-torn Sudan, the figure soars to 2.7 percent, and Libya's population is growing at an annual rate of 2.4 percent. Only small Tunisia, growing at 1.1 percent, has a RNI comparable to the world average.

Southwest Asia, with an annual 2.1 percent RNI, is growing even more rapidly than is North Africa. Palestinian Territory holds the distinction of having the world's highest reproduc-tive rate—an explosive 3.4 percent. Israel, with a population of about 7.1 million and RNI of 1.6 percent, is rapidly losing demographic ground to the Palestinians. This reality holds serious political as well as demographic implications for this troubled part of the world. Yemen ranks right behind the Pal-estinians with a 3.3 percent annual growth. Iraq, Saudi Arabia, and Syria all boast a 2.7 RNI, a full 1.5 percent above the world average. Within the entire North Africa and Middle Eastern region, every country except Tunisia is reproducing well above the world average. Of all the world's regions, only Africa south of the Sahara is reproducing more rapidly.

OTHER DEMOGRAPHIC MEASURES

Demography is defined as "the statistical study of the human population." In addition to populations and population growth rates, there are many other kinds of data that are important to geographers. Birth and death rates, for example, can tell us a great deal about a country or region. They reveal conditions of health care and sanitation, economic conditions, levels of educational attainment, and much more. Throughout the region, birthrates rank among the world's highest. In fact, only four countries—Algeria, Morocco, Tunisia, and the United Arab Emirates—fall below the world average of 20 births per 1,000 population per year. Death rates, on the other hand are very low. Only strife-ridden Iraq and Sudan have death rates higher than the world average of 9 per 1,000. This huge gap between births and deaths explains the region's unusually high rate of natural population increase.

The gap between birth and death rates also helps explain why there are so many young people in the region. Worldwide, about 29 percent of the population is under 15 years of age, and 7 percent is 65 years or older. In North Africa and the Middle East, the figures are 35 percent and 4 percent, respectively. In Sudan, 44 percent of the population is under 15 years of age, and only 2 percent is 65 or older. Iraq ranks closely behind: About 42 percent of the population in this strife-ridden land is 15 or younger, and only 3 percent of the people have reached age 65.

Life expectancy is defined as the number of years one can expect to live at birth. Worldwide, men live an average 65 years and women 69 years, for an average life expectancy of 67 years. Figures for North Africa and the Middle East are identical and fall very close to the world averages. Throughout the region as a whole, men live an average 66 years and women 70 years, for an average life expectancy of 68 years.

SETTLEMENT

Settlement refers to where people live. Geographers want to know whether a population is tightly clustered or widely scattered across the land. Do most people live in rural or urban areas? Is migration occurring, and, if so, where are people moving to and from, and what factors influence their decision to migrate? These are just some of the settlement-related questions that must be answered in regard to a region's population distribution. Even a hurried glance at a population distribution map or the World at Night image will show that North Africa and the Middle East has a very tightly clustered population. Huge areas support hardly any human life. Where good water is available at the surface, however, huge populations exist in many locations.

The importance of a reliable source of good water in this otherwise parched landscape is a recurrent theme throughout this book. The United States and North Africa and the Middle East occupy roughly the same area. Yet amazingly, despite 90 percent of its land area being nearly void of people, the region is home to about 100 million more people than live in the United States!

Population Distribution and Density

Population density refers to the number of people living within a defined area (such as a square mile or square kilometer). The Palestinian Territory, for example, has 1,556 people per square mile (590 per square kilometer), which is one of the world's highest densities. Israel, with 875 people per square mile (330 per square kilometer), has the region's second greatest density. Knowing these density figures, you can better understand why the issue of land possession is so important to both Israelis and Palestinians. At the other extreme, Libya and Western Sahara have densities of only 8 and 4 people, respectively, per square mile (3 and 1.5 per square kilometer).

Unfortunately, rarely if ever are such figures realistic in terms of where people actually do (and do not) live. Egypt offers a wonderful example of why geographers rarely take population density figures seriously. The country has an area of about 387,000 square miles (1,000,000 square kilometers) and some 77 million people. Statistically, this gives Egypt a population density of just under 200 people per square mile (77 per square kilometer). This figure is well above the world's average density of 125 people per square mile (48 per square kilometer). But do these figures really tell you much about where Egypt's people actually live? Do they give you a realistic picture of how the population is actually distributed throughout the country's territory? On the World at Night image, notice the bright "line" of white indicating where the country's people live. They are densely clustered in the fertile valley oasis created by the Nile River. Here, in about 4 percent of the country's land area, population density reaches nearly 5,000 people per square mile (1,930 per square kilometer)! The remainder of the country, other than for a few scattered oases, is virtually uninhabited.

Similar conditions—although perhaps not to the extreme illustrated by Egypt—exist throughout most of the region. Amazingly, 13 countries within the region have population densities that exceed the world's average! As a general rule, however, it is safe to say that in most countries, the population is tightly packed. Roughly 90 percent of the people live in 10 percent or less of the land area. There are, of course, some exceptions. In Tunisia, Israel, Lebanon, Syria, and Turkey, most of the territory is effectively settled. Much of rural Iran is settled, as is the Mesopotamian region of Iraq. Much of Saudi Arabia is desert, and most of the territory of North African countries is within the bone-dry Sahara Desert. These lands, as they are actually referred to, are largely an "Empty Quarter" with very few people.

Rural Versus Urban Living

When thinking of North Africans and Middle Easterners, many Westerners hold the stereotypical image of pastoral nomads. To others, the region's typical resident is someone living in a small, remote, oasis settlement. Although nomads and small oasis villages still exist, for the vast majority of people living within the region, these images have been wrong for centuries. The Middle East is the cradle of urban living and is home to some of the world's earliest and most thriving cities. Today, the region's urban population ranks at or above the world average. Nearly one of every two North Africans lives in an urban area. In the Middle East, the figure rises to two-thirds of the population. In Kuwait, Qatar, and Israel, more than 90 percent of all people live in cities. In fact, only in rural Sudan and Yemen does the urban population fall below the world average of 50 percent.

There is a very close relationship between urban living and such conditions as levels of educational attainment, per-capita income, and "modern" living. Rural people throughout the world tend to have very traditional, conservative lifestyles that are tied to folk cultures. Urban people, on the other hand, tend to be much more receptive to change. The demands of urban life also call for different skills, including reading, writing, and mathematics. In addition, throughout most of the world (including North Africa and the Middle East), the rate of population increase declines rapidly as urban populations grow.

Geographers recognize many types of urban centers, including "primate cities." A primate city is one that dominates a country. It is the largest city (usually by a wide margin), typically the country's capital, and its most important economic and cultural center. Most countries in North Africa and the Middle East have a primate city that far overshadows all other urban centers. In Southwest Asia, Tehran (Iran), Baghdad (Iraq), Damascus (Syria), Tel Aviv (Israel), and Amman (Jordan) fulfill this role. Saudi Arabia and Turkey are the major exceptions. Riyadh is the Saudi capital and largest city, whereas Mecca is the nation's heart and cultural soul. Ankara is Turkey's capital, but Istanbul is its population, economic, and cultural center. With the exception of Morocco, all capital cities in North Africa are also primate centers that overwhelmingly dominate their respective country's affairs.

City populations are very difficult to determine with any accuracy. For example, Los Angeles, California, has a

North Africa and the Middle East has several primate cities, including Tel Aviv, Israel, the skyline of which is pictured here. Primate cities are the largest in their respective countries and typically serve as the capital and cultural and economic hub.

population of about 3.9 million within its political (legal) city limits. Within the Los Angeles metropolitan area (the city and all of its suburbs), however, the population soars to about 17.5 million. Which figure is correct for the "city's" population? These differences in population figures exist for many if not most of the cities in North Africa and the Middle East. In addition, the previously mentioned lack of reliable census data makes many urban population figures little more than guesses. What is known is that about 20 cities within the region have metropolitan populations exceeding one million. Cairo (Egypt) and Istanbul (Turkey) are the largest, each with populations estimated to be around 10 million, followed closely by Tehran (Iran). By any measure, these three huge metropolitan areas rank among the world's 20 largest urban centers.

MIGRATION

As is the case throughout much of the rest of the world, the region's cities are experiencing explosive population growth. Much of the gain is the result of in-migration, particularly from poor rural areas. When people move, they generally do so for economic reasons. By moving, they hope to make a better living and make their lives more comfortable and secure. For centuries, the primary migration pattern in North Africa and the Middle East, as well as throughout most of the rest of the world, has been from rural to urban. Rural life can be extremely difficult. Cities, throughout their history, have drawn people from the countryside. They appear to offer excitement, opportunity, security, amenities, and many other attractions. Cities offer better educational opportunities and health care, as well as more goods to purchase and a variety of jobs that provide the money with which to make purchases.

Some people migrate for reasons other than direct economic gain. Environmental conditions can deteriorate, resulting in a substantial out-migration from a region. This happened throughout much of the Sahel, the semiarid zone bordering the southern Sahara, during the severe drought of the 1970s and 1980s. War can cause massive adjustments in where people live. Many countries within the region have suffered recent civil conflicts, resulting in large migrations of people seeking a safe refuge. Nowhere has this occurred with more tragic results than in Sudan during recent decades. The sad situation in the former Palestine and present-day Israel is addressed elsewhere. Here, too, thousands of people—both Palestinians and Israelis—have been forced to relocate, often repeatedly.

Some countries within the region have a huge imbalance in the sexes, with many more males than females. Qatar, for example, has 1.88 males for every female, leading the world in this category. Bahrain, Kuwait, and the United Arab Emirates also have a very high ratio of males to females. These imbalances can easily be explained. The countries are very small, yet they have booming oil-based economies. As a result, they must import large numbers of male laborers, most of whom come from nearby Pakistan, India, and Bangladesh.

People, as has been proven time and time again, have the potential of being any region's most important resource. This is true throughout Western Europe, Northern America, Japan, and elsewhere. In order to contribute to society, however, individuals must be allowed to reach their true potential. No segment of society can be held back by the shackles of discrimination. All people must be free to advance within the limits of their capability. They must have access to a quality education, good health care, and capital resources. If a government is to prosper, its political and economic systems must provide security and ensure stability for its people. Unfortunately, North Africa and the Middle East has a long way to go before its citizens will be able to reach their human resource potential.

CHAPTER 7

Cultural Geography

From afar, North Africa and the Middle East may appear to be a region in which culture—peoples' language, religion, economic activity, government, and other aspects of living—is rather similar. Nothing could be further from the truth. For every cultural stereotype, there are many exceptions. Several examples, including the great diversity of languages and religions, were presented in some detail in Chapter 1. Attention in this chapter will focus on the most important aspects of the region's cultural patterns: religion, government, and economy.

RELIGION

The world's three great monotheistic faiths—Judaism, Christianity, and Islam (as well as several smaller faiths)—rose in the Middle East. Today,

Despite the fact that the world's three great monotheistic religions—Judaism, Christianity, and Islam—developed in the Middle East, the number of Muslim adherents dwarfs those of Christianity and Judaism. One exception is Lebanon, where 40 percent of the population practices Christianity. Pictured here is a procession of Lebanese Christians passing by the Mohammad al-Amin Mosque in Beirut on Palm Sunday.

Judaism remains a very small "island" in Israel, surrounded by a vast sea of Islamic dominance. Christians are found in very small numbers scattered throughout the region. Their greatest concentration is in Lebanon, where Christianity is practiced by about 40 percent of the population. Islam, the faith founded by the Prophet Muhammad in the seventh century, dominates the region by a wide margin. With the exception of Israel and Lebanon, most (more than 95 percent) of the region's people are Muslims. (Islam is the faith, and Muslims are its followers; it is incorrect to refer to either as Muhammadenism or Muhammadins.)

Islam

Although subtle and complex, like all religions, Islam's message and practice are simple and straightforward. The faith's beliefs are set forth in its most holy book, the Koran (*Qu'ran*), which is written in the Arabic language. (In fact, the Koran sets the standard for written Arabic.) Muslims believe in the Five Pillars (obligations) of Islam, which are stated in the Koran:

(1) *Shahadah*, or profession of faith: Allah is the one true God and Muhammad is the messenger of God;
(2) *Salah*, the call to prayer five times a day while facing toward Mecca;
(3) *Sadaqah*, the giving of alms to the needy;
(4) *Sawm*, fasting from dawn to sunset during the month of Ramadan;
(5) *Hajj*, a pilgrimage to Mecca, Islam's most holy city, at least once during one's lifetime, if able.

The Koran serves as the basis of *Sharia*—the sacred law of Islam. The Sharia covers all aspects of the lives of Muslims, including the spiritual, social, political, and economic, as well as public and private behavior.

Minarets, or tall, slender towers, are a dominant feature of communities throughout North Africa and the Middle East. These are the towers that rise above *mosques* that in times past a *muezzin* would climb five times daily to give the call to prayer. Today, however, the "hasten to prayer" call is most often made from a loudspeaker. Muslims pray toward Mecca, rather than "to the east." (The faithful who live in Iraq or Turkey, for example, will pray toward the south, whereas in Afghanistan they will pray toward the west, and so on.) The holy month of Ramadan falls during the ninth month of the Islamic calendar. Because it is based on lunar rather than solar cycles, the ninth month changes each year relative to the calendar used in most of the world. Once Ramadan begins, Muslims must not eat or drink between dawn and sunset. They also should refrain from smoking, lying, swearing, engaging in sexual activity, becoming angry, or other bad habits.

The *Hajj* is another very important event to all Muslims who are able to make the often strenuous, costly, and dangerous trip. This occurs during the twelfth lunar month and is the time when Muslims go to Islam's most holy site, the Kaaba (*Ka'ba*), in Mecca. Each year, several million faithful crowd into Mecca during this period in what has become one of the world's greatest short-term pilgrimages.

Islam and Society

Islam, with an estimated 1.3 to 1.4 billion followers, is the world's second-ranking faith behind Christianity. Because of the high rates of population increase in Muslim-dominated countries, it is also the world's fastest growing major religion.

As noted elsewhere, North Africa and the Middle East is a complex mosaic of ethnic groups—each with differing histories, values, and coping strategies. In recent years, it has been assumed that a struggle exists between religion and nationalism (devotion to national interests and unity) as the principal cohesive force in society. For many years, Westernizing or modernizing trends in law, education, and other institutions were regarded as inevitable. "Progress" was expressed in secular, rather than religious, terms. In recent years, however, this trend appears to have been reversed throughout much of the region. Islamic beliefs are rising in strength to become the framework for the integration of social, economic, and political activity. In large measure, this represents a reaction to the unwelcome intrusions of the "West" into the affairs of the region.

Still, changes continue to take place. It is now clear that the contest is not simply one between religion and nationalism. Rather, it results from the dynamic interaction of religion, nationalism, ethnicity, age, affinity to popular or traditional culture, and many other factors. In the most religiously orthodox communities, as well as the most secular, one finds differing views on even basic Islamic beliefs. In some societies, for example, laws regarding diet and alcohol are strictly enforced, whereas in others they are quite relaxed. Required traditions of hospitality are often maintained in rural areas but are extended with reluctance in urban settings. Although judged "unclean" by traditional Islamic teachings, dogs are becoming increasingly popular pets in several Islamic societies. (Dogs used for hunting, guarding, or herding have long been valued, however.) Although the religious equality of men and women is affirmed in the Koran, equality in marriage, inheritance, education, and other important areas has long been unbalanced. Reform movements throughout North Africa and the Middle East are now addressing these issues.

The drive for change and reform in North Africa and the Middle East is widespread. Attacks on religion can still be a powerful rallying cry in the Islamic world. Nonetheless, there seems to be a movement toward a middle ground between the orthodoxy of an Islamic brotherhood and those who prefer more secular approaches to life and government. Some, for example, have favored a culturally "authentic" Islamic socialism. In any case, even those who reject Islam often retain Islamic habits and attitudes, and introduced values and ideologies are seldom permanent. Hence, an understanding of Islam is necessary to understand the region and its people today.

GOVERNMENT AND POLITICS

Good government is essential to economic development and human well-being. Yet for decades, most countries of North Africa and the Middle East have suffered from poor leadership. Many countries, in fact, have been ravaged by conflict, often leading to all-out war either internally, or with neighbors. Few countries have enjoyed a democratic political system or a stable government elected by and responsible to the people. Most countries within the region claim to be republics, but in reality this status is in name only. There are very few true democracies. Israel,

Egypt, and Turkey are among the small handful of countries in which democratic processes seem to have taken root. With the support of the United States and its allies, democratic government has been introduced to Afghanistan and Iraq. It is far too early, however, to determine whether this political experiment will be successful. Many countries, such as Saudi Arabia, Jordan, and Qatar, are ruled by a monarchy, or ruling family. A small number of states, such as Iran (and Afghanistan, under the former rule of the Taliban), are theocracies under the rule of Islamic leaders. Finally, a state of anarchy prevails in Somalia, where no government leads the country and it lies in chaos.

Today, a number of forces, some operating from outside and others from within, are playing a strong role in shaping local politics. Certainly, the wave of religious fundamentalism that is sweeping across much of the region is exerting a strong influence on governments. The movement, called "Political Islam," appears to be gaining support. It is fueled by Islamic leaders seeking not only individual political power, but for their countries to be under the rule of *Sharia* (Islamic law, or the law of Allah).

A second major influence, this one largely imposed by outside interests, is what can be called "petroleum politics." For at least a century, petroleum has fueled much of the world's industry, vehicles, and economy—and North Africa and the Middle East is home to most of this precious natural resource. Because of petroleum's importance to the global economy, it is little wonder that outside interests attempt to gain the favor of, or even control of, regional governments. U.S. involvement (and that of its allies) in Iraq is but the latest in a long history of outside meddling in regional political affairs.

In his 1980 State of the Union Address, President Jimmy Carter forcefully stated America's "petro-policy" in what has become known as the Carter Doctrine. Although then directed at the Soviet Union, Carter said, "Any attempt by an outside force to gain control of the Persian Gulf region will be regarded as an assault on the vital interests of the United States of America."

Obviously, both Democrat and Republican leaders recognize the vital importance of this region to the industrial world. Although Carter was warning off aggression from outside the region, his words have led recent administrations to involve themselves in regional conflicts. During recent years, for example, the United States and its allies have been involved in military engagements in Kuwait, Afghanistan, and Iraq. The West also views Iran's growing nuclear capability as an ominous threat to regional, if not global, stability.

AGRICULTURAL ECONOMY

Traditionally, economic activity in North Africa and the Middle East was dominated by sedentary oasis agriculture and pastoral nomadism. Today, both subsistence farmers and nomadic herders are declining in number and importance. In most countries, these folk practices have given way to petroleum, manufacturing, and services as the leading contributors to national economies.

Most scientists believe that agriculture began in North Africa and the Middle East. Not only was the region a major hearth of plant and animal domestication, but it also has a long history of experimentation and adaptation that has resulted in highly developed systems of production. In some areas, for example, underground aqueducts deliver groundwater from distant highlands to gardens and fields. Deep-basin systems permit farmers to plant crops in soils from which salts have been removed by an elaborate system of flooding and evaporation. Water-harvesting techniques permit other farmers to grow crops in arid regions, without recourse to conventional irrigation. Many of these innovative techniques are described in ancient agriculturalist books, such as *Geoponika*, and can still be seen today during an excursion to the countryside. In some areas, poor farming practices have seriously affected agricultural production; in others, productivity significantly exceeds the world average for many crops.

Prior to the development of the petroleum industry, much of the region's economy was dominated by agriculture. Despite the

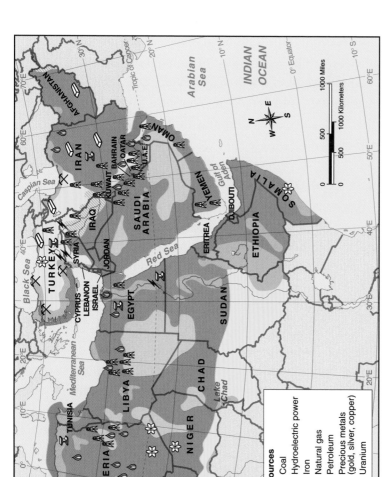

Land Use

- ☐ Subsistence farming
- ☐ Commercial farming
- ☐ Nomadic herding
- ☐ Commercial fishing
- ☐ Forestry
- ☐ Trade and manufacturing
- ☐ Little or no activity

Resources

- ⚒ Coal
- ⚡ Hydroelectric power
- ⚒ Iron
- ◈ Natural gas
- ⚒ Petroleum
- ⬡ Precious metals (gold, silver, copper)
- ✺ Uranium

The economy of North Africa and the Middle East has traditionally been based on farming and herding. However, the region contains vast amounts of mineral resources, including oil, coal, and natural gas.

modest precipitation, many farmers depend entirely on rainfall to produce their crops. This rain-fed agriculture, or "dry farming," is typically associated with grain crops, such as wheat, barley, oats, and millet. Rain-fed agriculture is particularly important in northwestern Morocco, on the high plateaus of Algeria and Anatolia, the Syrian steppes, and the Fertile Crescent, as well as in the relatively well-watered highlands of Iran and Afghanistan. Highly specialized methods of obtaining water, using rubble mulches to reduce evaporation and terracing hillsides, and other measures have been practiced for thousands of years. Terracing, often associated with East Asia, was widely used in mountainous areas of Morocco, Lebanon, Yemen, Sudan, and elsewhere.

Irrigated agriculture is also widespread in North Africa and the Middle East. Water sources include rivers, groundwater sources, and springs. Among the most ancient forms of irrigated farming is recessional agriculture. As floodwaters recede, crops are simply planted in the damp earth. This has been a particularly effective form of agriculture. Floodwaters are typically of high quality, and they also wash away any salts that might have accumulated in the floodplain soils. Groundwater also supports irrigated agriculture. In antiquity, hand-dug wells as deep as 400 feet (120 meters) were not unusual and were typically the work of guild specialists. Modern wells have been drilled into aquifers as deep as 3,000 feet (915 meters).

Unfortunately, mechanical pumps often extract groundwater more rapidly than it is replenished. Hence, many agricultural communities dependent on groundwater are facing severe shortages. Along the banks of rivers and lakes, as well as in oasis agriculture, a number of ancient devices were employed to lift water for irrigating crops. They include the counter-poised sweep (*shaduf*), the waterwheel (*noria*), and a screw within a cylinder used to raise water a few feet from one level to another (Achimedes' screw). In areas of sufficient warmth, the use of these devices permitted the development of multiple-cropping systems that extended production well into the dry season. The subterranean aqueducts described earlier date from the third millennium B.C. Evidence suggests that they first appeared in Minoan Crete and then spread throughout the drylands of North Africa and the Middle East. They have the advantage of providing irrigation water of high quality throughout the year.

In the more recent past, dams have diverted or impounded river water, making it available for irrigation during the dry season. Unfortunately, irrigation has often resulted in water-logging or salinization (salt buildup in the soil). The practice also contributes to increased water-borne disease, greater concentrations of agricultural chemicals in rivers and lakes, and other changes that disrupt the ecology of the river basin. In some areas, river-basin development projects have also resulted in agricultural expansion into areas of seasonal importance to pastoral nomads. This has destroyed the nomadic system of livelihood in some locations.

In addition to grain crops, the farmers of North Africa and the Middle East are engaged in arboriculture (tree crops), viticulture (grape cultivation), and growing a broad range of vegetables and other crops. Tree crops include dates; nuts, such as almonds, walnuts, and pistachios; olives; soft fruits, such as figs, apricots, peaches, plums, pears, and cherries; and citrus—particularly oranges, lemons, and tangerines. Iran is the leading producer of tree crops, followed by Turkey. Grapes are also important in the region, as are bananas grown in southern Turkey, Lebanon, and Israel. Garden crops are diverse and plentiful and, because they are locally grown, they are fresh and flavorful. Industrial crops include cotton, sugar beets and sugar cane, tobacco, linseed, hemp, and sunflowers. The high-rainfall areas of Turkey's Black Sea coast and Iran's Caspian lowlands also produce tea, rice, hazelnuts (filberts), and corn. Yemen's highlands are famous for coffee production, as well as for *qat*, a controversial narcotic used as a stimulant. Other narcotic crops include opium poppies, grown under government control in Turkey and Iran and grown illegally in Afghanistan. Hashish is also grown illegally in Lebanon and Iran.

Despite its challenges, livestock grazing remains an important economic activity in the region. Village-based animal husbandry includes animals such as cattle, horses, donkeys, mules, camels, goats, and sheep. They are used for meat and milk, raw materials (such as fertilizer and wool), as beasts of burden, and for transportation. Various forms of poultry also contribute to village economies. Most animals in the region, however, are held by pastoral nomads. The most common herd animals in arid areas are goats, sheep, donkeys, and camels. Water permitting, cattle are often prominent herd animals, as well. Herd composition is determined by environmental factors, social status, and economic considerations.

Pastoral nomads often cover considerable distances, with patterns of movement influenced chiefly by the availability of forage and water. The two principal forms of nomadism are transhumance (vertical movement) in mountainous areas and horizontal migration. In transhumance, herders follow traditional routes, alternating between winter pastures in the lowlands and summer pastures in the highlands—sometimes planting crops along the route. Nomads often establish relationships with lowland villages, with their livestock permitted into fields to consume crop residue after the harvest, thus contributing manure to fertilize the next season's crops. There is also an exchange of animal products for grain and other commodities desired by the nomads. Horizontal migration typically involves movement from one known well or other source of water to another. Livestock radiate outward from that source until water or forage conditions prompt the nomads to move on to a new location. Camels, goats, and sheep are generally favored by pastoral nomads following horizontal migratory paths in arid regions.

Although never representing more than maybe 10 percent of the region's population, pastoral nomadism has become even less widespread. Governments are often eager to settle nomads, because, historically, they are viewed as threats. Because they lack a permanent "address," they are often difficult to tax,

formally educate, or enroll in military service. Some governments even view nomads as embarrassing artifacts of the past.
As noted earlier, nomadic systems were also affected by agricultural expansion and the delineating of political boundaries that
often limited their range.

FORESTRY

Although few extensive forests exist in North Africa and the
Middle East today, historical evidence indicates that forests were
extensive in North Africa, the Levant, what is now the Syrian
Desert, and the plateau of Iran. There is even evidence from the
1700s of forests in the Arabian Peninsula. Today, the region's
most extensive forests extend through the Pontic and Taurus
mountains in western Anatolia to the Iranian border, and along
the northern slopes of the Elburz Mountains. The Anatolian
forests are dominated by oak and pine in the west and beech and
spruce in the east. In addition to beech, the Iranian forest contains linden, ash, oak, elm, walnut, maple, and various evergreens.
Remnants of the ancient forests still exist in several countries and
reforestation projects are found throughout the region. Iran's
reforestation efforts are particularly extensive, but noteworthy
projects exist in nearly every state in North Africa and the Levant.
Some projects, particularly those in Algeria and Abu Dhabi, have
established small forests in desert landscapes. Among the native
species involved in reforestation efforts are the Aleppo pine, oak,
pistachio, and tamarisk. Efforts to reestablish the cedars of Lebanon have met with some success, but have proven to be difficult.
Somewhat more attention should be given to increased efforts
in environmental rehabilitation, as well as to the restoration of
biological diversity. Turkey is the only country in the region with
a well-developed forest industry.

FISHERIES

North Africa and the Middle East borders numerous water
bodies, with coastlines that total 14,585 miles (23,470 kilometers).

Egypt is the leading country in fish landed, followed by Morocco, Turkey, and Iran. Egypt's lead has resulted from the increased productivity of its freshwater fishery. The Moroccan fishery benefits from the nutrient-rich cold water upwelling in the Atlantic Ocean. Turkey, in response to the issue of sustainability that plagues industrial fisheries, has successfully experimented with small-scale cooperative fishing ventures. This approach assures greater benefits to individuals and communities. It also is more ecologically sound and better protects fishery resources. Iran benefits from its access to both the Persian Gulf and the Gulf of Oman, as well as the Caspian Sea. Unfortunately, pollution and poaching have reduced the sturgeon catch in the Caspian, and with it the valuable harvest of caviar (fish roe, or eggs). Yemen, Oman, and the United Arab Emirates also maintain active fisheries. Similar to the Moroccan fishery, the Yemeni and Omani fisheries benefit from the rich, upwelling waters along the southern coast of the Arabian Peninsula. The fish harvest is threatened by industrial and agricultural pollution and severe overfishing by modern fleets. Nonetheless, during the early 2000s, all major fishing states of the region increased their catch.

MINING

North Africa and the Middle East possesses a variety of valuable minerals. Many minerals are found in small deposits, but larger deposits are also found in the region. For example, the phosphate deposits of Morocco are extensive and claim a large share of the world market. Northwestern Africa also possesses significant quantities of iron ore, manganese, lead, zinc, and uranium. Cyprus has long been an important source of copper, iron pyrites, and chromite, as well as gypsum, salt, marble, and asbestos. As is the case with agricultural production, Turkey and Iran are the leading states in the mining sector. They produce coal, chromite, copper, iron ore, lead, manganese, zinc, sulfur, and a variety of other minerals. Syria, Iraq, Jordan, Israel, and Egypt possess large reserves of phosphate, and Jordan and Israel produce significant quantities of potash from the Dead Sea. Oman and Afghanistan also possess a variety of valuable minerals. Oman produces copper, chromite, asbestos, marble, limestone, and gypsum; Afghanistan's mineral wealth includes copper, chromite, iron ore, barite, sulfur, lead, zinc, talc, salt, and a variety of gemstones.

OIL AND NATURAL GAS

Oil and natural gas are found throughout North Africa and the Middle East, although they are unevenly distributed. The largest reserves are found in and around the Persian Gulf. Saudi Arabia, Iran, Iraq, the United Arab Emirates, and Kuwait all have extensive deposits of these precious fossil fuels. In North Africa, Algeria and Libya also possess large reserves. Possessing more than 65 percent of the world's known reserves, these countries are of enormous economic and strategic importance to the industrialized countries of the world. A few countries, including Egypt, Syria, and Yemen, also possess sufficient reserves for domestic consumption. Although other countries produce some oil and gas, most find it necessary to import additional supplies in order to satisfy their needs. This is a situation somewhat similar to that of the United States. The United States is the third-largest producer of crude oil in the world, but finds it necessary to import about half of the oil that it consumes—more than 10 million barrels each day.

Little was known about the size of oil and natural gas reserves when the colonial powers laid claim to the region. The presence of these fossil fuels had been known for millennia, because of asphalt, natural gas, and oil seeps. Natural tars from the region were said to have been used in the construction of Noah's ark and served as mortar in the construction of Ur. Eternal flames are remembered in several Old Testament passages, including the "fiery furnace" of Shadrach. Oil from regional seeps was used to fuel lamps. William Knox D'Arcy, a British investor, obtained a concession to drill for oil in western Iran, where a major strike was made in 1908. Hence, it was known that oil and natural gas

Oil and natural gas were known to exist within the region of North Africa and the Middle East long before the colonial powers arrived. However, the discovery of vast amounts of oil in Iran in 1908 by the Anglo-Iranian Oil Company prompted a huge demand for this new source of fuel. Pictured here are workers at one of the first Anglo-Iranian Oil company derricks in 1909.

existed in the region, but the commercial demand for these commodities was not particularly great at the time.

The Iranian discovery led to the creation of the Anglo-Iranian Oil Company in 1909—a company that evolved into British Petroleum in 1951. The demand for oil rapidly increased in the early 1900s, when the British Navy switched to fuel oil for firing its boilers. The Turkish Petroleum Company, formed by British, French, and Dutch interests, discovered oil near Kirkuk in 1927. The United States initially became involved in the region through involvement with Turkish Petroleum in 1928. After that time, the scramble for the oil and gas reserves of the region began in earnest. It has involved countless intrigues. Helpful governments were empowered and those that resisted were often overthrown. Enormous fortunes were made by those in a position to benefit from oil production, but oil-related conflicts have also resulted in hundreds of thousands of deaths. Oil and natural gas have drawn Islamic societies into world affairs. Europe and the United States possessed the wealth and knowledge to exploit the energy resources of North Africa and the Middle East. With this expertise came the "vulgarities" of Western popular culture that are resisted by Islamic traditionalists. More than in the past, nonpolitical (often religious) militancy is rising to oppose Western dominance in the region.

Geographers Harm J. deBlij and Peter Muller describe the principal impacts of oil as follows:

- **High Incomes.** Several of the oil-producing states are among the wealthiest in the world.

- **Modernization.** Large oil revenues have transformed cultural landscapes throughout the realm, producing a façade of modernization.

- **Industrialization.** Several states are investing in industrialization, with the knowledge that the oil and natural gas will at some point be depleted.

- **Intrarealm Migration.** Oil wealth has attracted millions of workers from less favored parts of the region to work in the oil fields, ports, and service activities.

- **Interrealm Migration.** Oil wealth has also attracted workers from states beyond the region: from Pakistan, India,

Sri Lanka, and other states. Competition for jobs and diversity has increased the control that North African and Middle Eastern governments have over the workforce.

- **Regional Disparities.** Oil wealth and its manifestations in the cultural landscape create strong contrasts with areas not directly affected. For example, the ultramodern east coast of Saudi Arabia is a world apart from large areas of its interior.

- **Foreign Investment.** Governments and Arab business owners have invested oil-generated wealth in foreign countries. These investments created networks of international involvement that linked the region to the economies of foreign states. It is clear that oil and natural gas have benefited some people within the region, just as it has dislocated and imperiled others.

INDUSTRY

North Africa and the Middle East has a long history of manufacturing high-quality goods. Nonetheless, by international standards, the region has been relatively slow to develop industrially. (One noteworthy exception, of course, is petroleum refining.) Exports include textiles from Turkey, Egypt, and Israel; clothing from the Levant and United Arab Emirates; wines from Algeria, the Levant, and Cyprus; and processed foods from Morocco and Syria. Israel is a leading exporter, producing cut diamonds, electronics, software, and armaments. The petrochemical plants of the Gulf States are similarly oriented toward export. In terms of value-added manufacturing, Turkey is the most productive state in the region. Iraq was formerly a regionally significant industrialized state, but much of its industrial capacity was lost during recent military engagements. Turkey, Iran, and Egypt have the largest number of industrial workers, and Turkey and Iran have the greatest number of enterprises.

Apart from the export economy, virtually every state is engaged in the production of processed foods, beverages, and cigarettes. They also produce construction materials, metalwork, textiles, clothing, leather products, woodwork, ceramics, jewelry, and printed materials. States rich in oil and natural gas have been able to apply these resources to water distillation, the generation of electricity, aluminum smelting, and other energy-intensive undertakings. In the most heavily industrialized North African and Middle Eastern states, there are industries engaged in the assembling of motor vehicles, ships, major appliances, electronic items, machine tools, and armaments. Many of these activities are directly linked to foreign corporations.

TRANSPORTATION

The Dutch, Portuguese, and British, in succession, controlled the region's sea lanes after the sixteenth century and before World War II. Because transportation in the region was historically linked to the maritime and caravan trades, roads were largely unnecessary. In 1859–1863, however, a French company constructed a road linking Beirut to Damascus. In 1869, the Suez Canal linked the Red Sea with the Mediterranean. The 101-mile (163-kilometer) canal was cut through Egypt's Isthmus of Suez, thereby shaving approximately 12,000 miles (19,300 kilometers) from the long, costly, and hazardous trip around Africa.

By the early 1900s, the French, British, Germans, and Russians had become involved in the construction of roads, railroads, and ports throughout the region. These facilities often were built to support their own commercial or administrative interests. By the late 1920s, a relatively complete transportation infrastructure was in place, and it was significantly improved by the end of World War II. From the 1950s, income from oil and natural gas, as well as support from international agencies, helped finance the building of a regional network of roads, seaports, airports, pipelines, and railroads. An extensive transportation infrastructure, including highways and railroads, as well as air and water transportation, is now in place in North Africa and the Middle East. Dubai has become a major international airline hub and boasts one of the world's top-ranked airports based on passenger preference.

TOURISM

Tourism forms another link to the global economy. Few areas of the world can match North Africa and the Middle East in potential attractions. It is home to a broad array of fascinating natural wonders, ranging from parched desert landscapes to tree- (and often snow-) clad mountains. Seas, oceans, rivers, and oases each offer potential for tourist development. The region's countless historical and religious sites are well known, as is its rich and varied cultural heritage. Great cities, exotic shopping, and wonderful food are other attractions.

Opportunities for recreation attract tourists to the region's beaches. Increasingly, adventure tourism, ecotourism, and cultural tourism are also attracting visitors interested in snorkeling in the Red Sea, observing birds and wildlife, or migrating with Iranian pastoral nomads. The range of possible activities is enormous. Tourism is already of considerable importance to the economies of Turkey, Israel, and Egypt. As the range of options increases and tourist facilities expand, tourism certainly will gain in economic importance throughout much of the region. Tourism has its benefits, but it has disadvantages, as well. Tourists contribute to visual blight and may damage archaeological and environmental sites. The industry distributes its benefits unevenly, can create social disturbances, and can have other negative impacts. In turn, tourists are not going to travel where they feel threatened. Conditions throughout much of the region must stabilize before the huge economic potential of tourism can be fully realized.

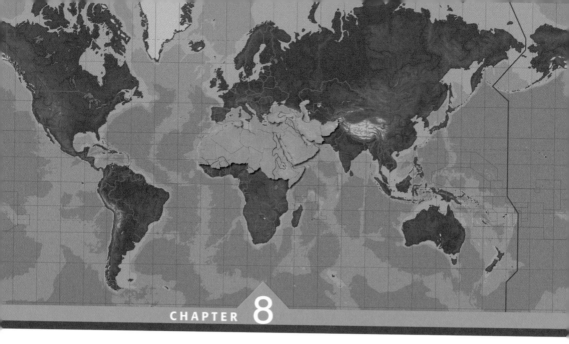

CHAPTER 8

A Troubled Region Looks Ahead

It is somewhat difficult to look ahead with great optimism in regard to the future of North Africa and the Middle East. The region can look back on a past that was in many ways glorious. It was home to the dawn of agriculture, the world's earliest cities, and giant leaps forward in science and technology. Written languages and mathematics were developed in response to the record-keeping needs of specialized urban societies. Some of the world's great early trade routes and market centers were located within the region. And, of course, it was home to the world's three great monotheistic religions. Through the corridors of time, it was also home to many of the world's most romantic places, including six of the seven Wonders of the Ancient World. Numerous great empires rose, spread, and eventually withered away. We, of course, look to the region as the Cradle of Western Civilization. Today, however, the region is saddled with many problems, and its future is in doubt.

In order to understand many of the things that are happening (or not happening, as the case may be) in North Africa and the Middle East today, it is essential to understand the importance of history. Geographer Erhard Rostlund noted that "the present is the fruit of the past and contains the seeds of the future." Today, the region and its people are justifiably frustrated. They can only wonder what series of events contributed to their decline as a global power. What cultural dynamics allowed much of the rest of the world—and particularly the West—to eclipse them in strength and influence? Here, a clue from the past will also pro-vide a possible hint of the future.

Many of the region's people remain quite traditional in terms of their outlook and worldview. Millions of them are still under-going the transition from a traditional and primarily rural folk culture to a contemporary dominantly urban popular culture. Ties to the past provide security and comfort. Their religion, customs, traditions, and ways of day-to-day living have long provided them with a sense of security. The future, on the other hand, appears threatening. Outside influences—such as Western media, dress, and customs—often conflict sharply with many of their most fundamental values. Looking ahead, they are also confronted by a sometimes bewildering array of changes that can easily erode the very foundation of their social and cultural systems. Economically, much of the vast wealth from petroleum is siphoned off by distant corporations, or fills the coffers of a handful of powerful local aristocrats. Politically, most of the region's people have little say in how they are governed. In turn, many governments, themselves, feel threatened by outside forces. They fear losing their grip on power, should a wave of democracy sweep across the region.

At the same time, there are reasons for optimism. North Africa and the Middle East is potentially rich in human resources.

For this potential to be reached, however, all members of society—including women—must be treated as equals. For some time to come, much of the region can draw from its wealth of petroleum and natural gas to fuel the economy. A much greater portion of this revenue, however, must be used to further local development. Economic potentials, such as manufacturing and service industries, must be greatly expanded, along with transportation infrastructure, education, health care, and other social services. People must be given a much stronger voice in how they are governed. Fortunately, there are some signs that this is occurring. Many local and regional conflicts must be resolved before the region can be stabilized and begin working to achieve its full potential. Fortunately, history reveals many examples of seemingly insurmountable hurdles that have been overcome. Each of these hurdles can be surmounted with good leadership, regional cooperation, and the will of the people.

Looking ahead, the following factors or conditions appear to hold the greatest significance in determining the region's future:

1. **Israel's permanence as a nation must be recognized and accepted.**

   No issue is more important to regional stability than is a satisfactory resolution of the Arab/Palestinian-Israeli conflict. Israel will always be the source of deep antagonism within the region, but its existence as a nation must be accepted. Palestinians, too, must be better integrated into the regional economy. In this conflict, neither side is going to vanish.

2. **The importance of "oil politics" within the region will continue to grow.**

   Cultural and economic growth depends on energy, and much of today's global economy is powered by petroleum. North Africa and the Middle East contains an estimated two-thirds of the world's known petroleum reserves. The world's growing dependence on oil will surely be a major

One of the most important factors in determining North Africa and the Middle East's future is the resolution of the Arab/Palestinian-Israeli conflict. Many Israelis, such as this group of peace activists who are attending a rally in front of former Israeli prime minister Ariel Sharon's residence in September 2005, support peace talks between Palestinian and Israeli leaders.

factor in shaping the region's political future. Currently, the United States and its allies are attempting to stabilize the region while introducing democracy. It is far too early even to guess whether this attempt will be successful. With or without democratic governments, however, the industrial world will continue to play a very important role in regional "oil politics."

3. **Locally imposed conditions will continue to hinder economic growth and social stability**.

Deeply entrenched governments and the power elites who run them will be very reluctant to give up their control.

Current political and social structures greatly hinder economic diversification and growth within the region. As a result, the region is threatened by continued decline in regional economic strength relative to the developed world (and increasingly, much of the less-developed world). Socioeconomically, most countries within the region are greatly polarized: Most wealth is in the hands of a very small number of people. Certainly, the future will bring considerable upheaval to many countries tightly governed by family or other totalitarian rulers. People will seek better lives, more power, and a greater share of their country's wealth.

4. **Regional frustrations will continue to grow.**

   Change usually comes very slowly within traditional societies. Unless substantial improvements occur within regional, social, political, and economic conditions, frustrations will continue to grow. As we already have seen, mounting frustrations can contribute to terrorism. In this context, it must be remembered that deadly acts of terrorism are being conducted not only worldwide, but within the Islamic world, as well. Mounting frustration and resulting terrorism appear to recognize no boundaries.

5. **Islamic fundamentalism will continue to expand.**

   There are few signs that Islamic fundamentalism—including "political Islam," terrorism, or the desire to impose Sharia (Islamic law) upon other people—will diminish in the foreseeable future. It can only be hoped that religious leaders and other responsible parties can play a more positive role in guiding the actions of their followers.

6. **Tourism holds great potential for the region.**

   After oil, tourism holds the greatest potential for stable economic growth throughout much of the region. Few regions of the world have more to offer a visitor. Among its many attractions are some of the world's most unique natural landscapes, a rich and fascinating history, numerous ancient wonders, and a warm and charming people. Unfortunately, tourism is declining throughout much of the region. Until conditions become stabilized and travelers can be assured of their safety, this potential source of revenue will continue to be lost.

7. **North Africa and the Middle East will continue to be a focal point of global political attention.**

   Because of their dependence on oil, the governments of both developed and developing economies will become increasingly involved in the region's affairs. The United States, in particular (regardless of the political party in office), will continue to play a major role. As a result, internal resentment of outside influences may actually escalate.

8. **The region faces a post-petroleum crisis.**

   Oil-rich countries have depended almost exclusively on petroleum exports to sustain their economies. Enormous wealth has flowed into the coffers of the power elite, but in many countries, little if any attention has been given to developing other sectors of the economy. It is not known how long the oil reserves will last, perhaps it will only be several more decades. Developing other sectors of an economy—such as agriculture, industry, tourism, and various services—can take a very long time. Many countries will face a major economic crisis when their oil reserves become depleted. For many countries, there is no greater need than to begin developing alternative economic sectors immediately.

9. **During the foreseeable future, North Africa and the Middle East will be the world's most critical political, social, economic, and military "hot spot."**

   Existing social, political, and economic conditions are not conducive to developing regional stability. Neither are contemporary trends within Islam, including its political arm and associated terrorism. Until such time as the region's petroleum resources vanish, the region will continue to be a focal point of considerable international interest and pressure.

Ultimately, the future of North Africa and the Middle East rests with the people themselves. At the root of the region's problems (as is true of many other regions) lie corrupt, inept, ineffective governments that care little about the people they govern. "People," it is often stated, "get the government they deserve." Are we to believe that people of this region really deserve to be politically repressed? Considering current conditions, it is difficult to imagine political change coming anytime soon, or without great conflict. Might the same not have been said, though, about much of Latin America or the Soviet Union several decades ago? Outside influences—such as U.S. involvement in Afghanistan and Iraq—can assist in guiding change, but change ultimately must come from within. The people, themselves, must chart and travel their own route of destiny. Hopefully, the people will rise to the challenge and work together toward building a future in which all of this fascinating region's people can participate, thrive, and enjoy the full benefits of living.

7,000,000 YBP	Early human ancestors roam North Africa.
29,000	Neanderthals disappear.
18,500	Early agriculture is practiced in Nile Valley.
12,000	Sheep and goats join the dog as domesticated animals.
8,000	Cattle are domesticated.
7,500	Rising global sea level floods Black Sea basin.
6,000	Horse is domesticated.

B.C.

3500	Cities emerge in the Middle East.
2800	Abstract writing is developed.
2680	Construction of massive pyramids begins in Egypt.
2334	Sumer, weakened by conflict, falls to the armies of Sargon of Akkad.
1800	Iron used by Hittites on Anatolian Peninsula.
1674	Hyksos rise and dominate the Nile Delta.
1550	Hyksos are driven from Egypt.
1500	Thíra (Santoríni) erupts violently in eastern Mediterranean; Minoan civilization on island of Crete declines.
1138	Violent earthquake kills an estimated 230,000 people in Aleppo, Syria.
814	Carthage is established.
330–320	Alexander the Great conquers lands eastward, to create a vast empire.
31	Roman Empire is established.

A.D.

622	Prophet Muhammad departs from Mecca for Medina; the journey is called *Hegira.*
711	Muslims invade the Iberian Peninsula.
1095	First of many Crusades (that would last for three centuries) attempts to free Holy Land from Muslim control.

1300	Ottoman Empire comes to power; it lasts until early 1900s.
1346	Bubonic plague (Black Death) reaches Middle East from Europe, causing widespread deaths.
1869	Suez Canal opens.
1870s	First oil wells in the Caspian Basin are drilled.
1880s	Jews begin migrating back to Palestine (Israel) as part of the Zionist movement.
1908	Oil is discovered and wells are drilled in Iran.
1918	World War I ends; much of North Africa and the Middle East is partitioned into countries, most of which are established as European colonies.
1922	Violent rainstorms destroy Tamanrasset, in the central Saharan Ahaggar; Temperature reaches 136°F (58°C) at Al 'Aziziyah, Libya.
1948	Jewish state of Israel is created.
1980–1988	Iraq and Iran wage war against one another.
1990	Iraq invades Kuwait, and the United States and its allies intervene in what came to be known as the "Gulf War."
1991	Collapse of Soviet Union changes global geopolitical strategies.
2001	United States and its allies invade Afghanistan to remove Taliban government.
2003	Estimated 43,200 people die in earthquake that strikes southeastern Iran; United States and its allies invade Iraq, removing Saddam Hussein in an attempt to bring political stability to the country.
2005	Estimated 80,000 people die in earthquake that strikes northern Pakistan and neighboring areas of Afghanistan.

Aramco World. Published bimonthly by the Saudi Aramco Oil Company. Excellent source of articles on the Muslim-Arab world.

Bagnold, R. A. *The Physics of Blown Sand and Desert Dunes*. London: Methuen, 1941.

Beaumont, Peter, Gerald Henry Blake, and J. Malcolm Wagstaff. *The Middle East: A Geographical Study*. New York: Halsted Press, 1988.

Briggs, Lloyd Cabot. *Tribes of the Sahara*. Cambridge: Harvard University Press, 1960.

Cloudsley-Thompson, J. L., ed. *Sahara Desert*. Oxford: Pergamon Press, 1984.

Cressey, George B. *Crossroads: Land and Life in Southwest Asia*. Chicago: J. B. Lippincott Company, 1960.

de Blij, H.J. and Peter O. Muller. *Geography: Realms, Regions, and Concepts*. Hoboken, N.J.: John Wiley & Sons, 2004.

Gautier, E. F. *Sahara, The Great Desert*. New York: Columbia University Press, 1935.

Held, Colbert C. *Middle East Patterns: Places, Peoples, and Politics*. Boulder, CO: Westview Press, 1989.

Hills, E. S., ed. *Arid Lands: A Geographical Appraisal*. London: Methuen, 1966.

Leone, Bruno. *The Middle East: Opposing Viewpoints*. Saint Paul, MN: Greenhaven Press, 1982.

Lewis, Bernard. *The Arabs in History*. New York: Harper & Row, 1960.

Longrigg, Stephen H. *The Middle East: A Social Geography*. Chicago: Aldine Publishing Company, 1963.

Spencer, William. *The Middle East*. Global Studies Series. Dubuque, IA: McGraw-Hill/Dushkin, annual editions.

Walton, K. *The Arid Zones*. London: Hutchinson University Library, 1969.

JEFFREY A. GRITZNER is chairman of the Department of Geography, the Asian Studies Program, and the International and Cultural Diversity Cluster at the University of Montana. He spent two years in Iraq as a Peace Corps Volunteer in the early 1960s, two years in Chad, and eight months traveling throughout much of the Sahara Desert and Southwest Asia. Both his master's thesis and doctoral dissertation were on topics drawn from this region. He has done extensive research and consulting on topics relating to environmental issues in North Africa.

Coauthor and series editor CHARLES F. GRITZNER is distinguished professor of Geography at South Dakota State University in Brookings. He is now in his fifth decade of college teaching, research, and writing. In addition to teaching, he enjoys writing, working with teachers, and sharing his love of geography with readers. As the consulting editor for Chelsea House's MODERN WORLD CULTURES and MODERN WORLD NATIONS series, he has a wonderful opportunity to combine each of these hobbies. Gritzner has served as both president and executive director of the National Council for Geographic Education and has received the Council's highest honor, the George J. Miller Award for Distinguished Service to Geographic Education.